© Copyright 2021 - All rights reserved.

The content contained within this book may not be reproduced, duplicated or transmitted without direct written permission from the author or the publisher.

Under no circumstances will any blame or legal responsibility be held against the publisher, or author, for any damages, reparation, or monetary loss due to the information contained within this book, either directly or indirectly.

Legal Notice:

This book is copyright protected. It is only for personal use. You cannot amend, distribute, sell, use, quote or paraphrase any part, or the content within this book, without the consent of the author or publisher.

Disclaimer Notice:

Please note the information contained within this document is for educational and entertainment purposes only. All effort has been executed to present accurate, up to date, reliable, complete information. No warranties of any kind are declared or implied. Readers acknowledge that the author is not engaged in the rendering of legal, financial, medical or professional advice. The content within this book has been derived from various sources. Please consult a licensed professional before attempting any techniques outlined in this book.

By reading this document, the reader agrees that under no circumstances is the author responsible for any losses, direct or indirect, that are incurred as a result of the use of the information contained within this document, including, but not limited to, errors, omissions, or inaccuracies.

Table of Contents

What is Macro Diet? 5

    Carbohydrates 5

    Protein 6

    Fat 6

Benefits of Macro Diet 7

Breakfast and Brunch Recipes 8

    Tempeh Scramble with Spinach and Carrots ... 8

    Overnight Oats 9

    Kale Mozzarella Wrap 10

    Feta Egg Muffins 11

    Frittata 13

    Baked Eggs and Zoodles 14

    Tortilla with Zucchini 15

    Lime Poppy Seed Muffins 16

    Egg and Veggie Breakfast Bowl 17

    Green Shakshuka 18

Poultry Recipes 19

    Beans and Chicken Stir Fry 19

    Mushroom and Chicken 20

    Baked Ranch Chicken 22

    Turkey Burgers with Savory Warm Relish 23

    Pesto Chicken and Veggies 24

    Easy Turkey Salad 25

    Chipotle Chicken Bowl 26

    Turkey Parmesan Zucchini Boats 27

    Roasted Garlic & Herb Chicken and Veggies . 28

    Lemon Basil Chicken 29

Fish and Seafood Recipes 30

    Moroccan Salmon 30

    Simple Salmon Chowder 31

    Sweet and Sour Tuna 32

    Baked Cod with Tomatoes & Basil 33

    Zucchini Noodles and Lemon Shrimp ... 34

    Ceviche 35

    Spicy Shrimp and Sautéed Kale 36

    Quick and Easy Salmon Cakes 37

    Roasted Mustard Seed White Fish 38

    Baked Salmon Recipe with Asparagus & Yogurt Dill Sauce 39

Beef, Pork and Lamb Recipes 40

    Garlic Rosemary Pork Chops 40

    Spicy Pork 41

    Korean Ground Beef 42

    Sweet Ground Beef and Broccoli 43

    Beef Cannelloni 44

    Swiss chard & Artichoke Stuffed Pork Chops 45

    Pork Chops with Warm Lemon Vinaigrette 46

    Sriracha BBQ Ground Beef and Green Beans 47

    Grilled Lamb Chops 48

Roast Lamb 49

Vegetarian Mains Recipes 50

Chickpeas Meatball 50

Tomato Quinoa Soup with Roasted Chickpeas 51

Tofu Stir-Fry 52

Enchilada Zucchini Boats 53

Garlic Teriyaki Tempeh and Broccoli 54

Red Lentil Stew with Chickpeas 55

Grilled Cauliflower Steak 56

Cauliflower Fried Rice 57

Sweet Potato Chili 58

Avocado Pesto Zucchini Noodles 59

Salads, Snacks and Sides Recipes 60

Strawberry Caprese Pasta Salad 60

Lentil and Steak Salad 61

Green Bowl with Chicken 62

Turkey Avocado Cobb Salad 63

Beet and Pumpkin Salad 64

Avocado Chips 66

Jalapeño Pepper Egg Cups 67

Burger Fat Bombs 68

Cucumber Sushi 69

Bacon Asparagus Bites 70

Drinks and Beverages Recipes 71

Berry Avocado Breakfast Smoothie 71

Chocolate Peanut Butter Smoothie 72

Strawberry Zucchini Hemp Smoothie 73

Coconut Blackberry Mint Smoothie 74

Cucumber Green Smoothie 75

Nutmeg Strawberries Smoothie 76

Cauliflower Smoothie 77

Pumpkin Spice Smoothie 78

Lime Pie Smoothie 79

Coffee with Cream 80

Desserts Recipes 81

Chocolate Pudding Cake 81

Almond Cookies 82

Chocolate Raspberry Cheesecake 83

Nut Fudge 84

Almond Graham Crackers 85

Lemon Coconut Protein Balls 86

Berry Chocolate Mousses 87

Almond Barley Pudding 88

Peanut Butter Protein Cookies 89

Banana Protein Mug Cake 90

Four Weeks Meal Plan 91

1st Week 91

Second Week 92

Third Week 93

Fourth Week 94

Conclusion 95

What is Macro Diet?

The Macro Diet has grown in popularity in recent years, and people can eat any food that meets their daily macronutrient ("macro") requirement. Instead of just focusing on counting calories, the focus is on counting and tracking macronutrients. Some nutritionists believe that manipulating macronutrient intake can help people lose weight and meet their health and fitness goals.

The idea behind the Macro Diet is quite simple: Instead of staying below a calorie limit, focus on consuming a certain amount (usually grams) of macronutrients (protein, carbohydrates, and fat).

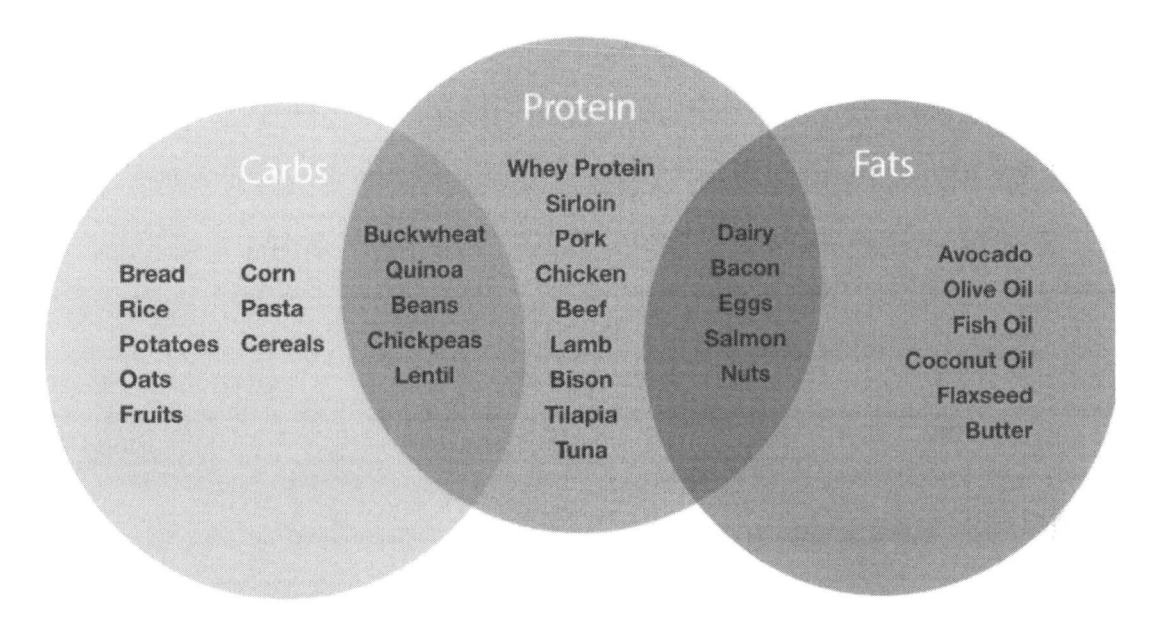

Protein
Whey Protein
Sirloin
Pork
Chicken
Beef
Lamb
Bison
Tilapia
Tuna

Carbs
Bread   Corn
Rice   Pasta
Potatoes Cereals
Oats
Fruits

Buckwheat
Quinoa
Beans
Chickpeas
Lentil

Fats
Avocado
Olive Oil
Fish Oil
Coconut Oil
Flaxseed
Butter

Dairy
Bacon
Eggs
Salmon
Nuts

Most foods contain two or even all three different macronutrients, but they are categorized by which macronutrient they contain the most. For example, chicken is a protein, although it is also low in fat, and sweet potatoes are considered carbohydrates despite being low in protein.

Carbohydrates

Carbohydrates are the main source of energy for the body. They are broken down into glucose (sugar) before being absorbed into the blood. They are needed to support the nervous system, kidneys, brain and muscles.

Sources of carbohydrates are found in all starches, like bread, rice, potatoes, pasta and breakfast cereals. Carbohydrates high in fiber, such as whole grains, release glucose into the blood more slowly than foods and drinks high in sugar.

Fiber is essential for overall health and lowers the risk of certain diseases such as colon cancer, heart disease, and type II diabetes. It also supports healthy digestion.

Healthy Sources of Carbohydrates Include:

- Fruits and vegetables
- Whole grains, such as brown rice
- Quinoa
- Whole grain bread
- Whole wheat pasta
- Potatoes

Protein

Protein is essential for building and maintaining body tissues, such as muscles, and it is also a source of energy. The main sources of protein are meat, fish, eggs, soy products, nuts and legumes.

Sources of High-Quality Protein Include:

- Fish, such as tuna and salmon
- Poultry, such as turkey and chicken breast
- Dairy products, such as milk, cheese, and yogurt
- Beans and legumes
- Nuts and seeds
- Tofu and soy products

Fat

Fat is essential for maintaining the normal structure of cells in the body. They also contain fat soluble vitamins, like vitamins A, D, E and K.

Sources of Healthy Fats Include:

- Olive or avocado oil
- Avocados
- Olives
- Nuts, such as walnuts, macadamias, and Brazil nuts
- Peanut butter
- Seeds, such as sunflower, sesame, chia, flax, and pumpkin

Benefits of Macro Diet

1. Helps you take responsibility for the right amount of food: A lot of people overeat if they don't watch carefully and take notes. And some, crazy as it sounds to many, don't eat enough unless they are responsible for a certain number of calories each day. In these cases, Macro Diet can be a great option to make sure you're getting the right number of calories for your goals, whether it's building muscle, losing fat, or recovering from a workout training.

2. It can be used in conjunction with certain diets to make sure your proportions are where they need to be: Ketosis and zone diets, for example, are both very accurate and require you to measure your macros so the percentages don't get lost. The benefit of the ketosis diet is that it trains your body to use fat as its primary source of energy, and consuming too much carbohydrate or protein can push you out of that fat burning and ketone production zone. Consume to reap your rewards.

3. Provides insight into any imbalances you may have with your current diet: As coaches we hear it all the time. "I eat properly" or "like a balanced diet". But what does it actually look like and are you really eating what you say and think you are eating? Once we start recording what we eat, we often find that certain things are happening or even missing. For example, people often think they are getting enough protein, but once they start writing on paper, they find out that they are not. Or others swear they "don't eat that much sugar," but according to their MyFitnessPal account – counting macros will help you spot these things.

4. Prevention of health problems: Some studies claim that tracking macronutrients can help prevent certain medical conditions. For example, there is some evidence that middle-aged adults who consume 6% of their daily calories from protein and increase that amount to 17% with age may protect themselves against Alzheimer's disease. Plus, eating a diet high in carbohydrates can help treat and protect against diabetes and cardiovascular disease. People may also want to see a doctor for nutritional advice if they have diabetes, vascular, or cardiovascular disease.

5. Open your eyes to the actual serving size: Unfortunately, for most of us, half a cup of peanut butter is much larger than the recommended serving. And the recommended serving of broccoli is way bigger than most of us would put on our plate... Oh yes, and the steaks you've eaten are probably two to three servings.

You can always make sure that you are eating right and building your body for success by following this simple rule. Eat real food and a variety of them! That means skipping processed foods and following these general rules for loading your plate: Mostly vegetables, a palm-sized serving of meat (or other protein), and a fat-sized serving. Add some post-workout strength and some fruit here and there.

Breakfast and Brunch Recipes

Tempeh Scramble with Spinach and Carrots

Prep time: 15 minutes
Cook time: 15 minutes
Serves: 4

Ingredients:

- 2 small carrots, cut into 1/2-inch cubes
- 2 tablespoons coconut oil
- 1 small yellow onion, chopped
- 2 14-ounce package tempeh, drained and crumbled
- ½ teaspoon garlic powder
- 2 teaspoons ground cumin
- 1 teaspoon salt
- ½ teaspoon turmeric
- 4 cups baby spinach
- Salt and pepper to taste

Preparation:

1. Place the carrots cubes in a large saucepan and cover with water. Bring it to a boil, then reduce the heat to medium and simmer for three minutes. Drain out all the water.
2. Add coconut oil and onion. Sauté over medium heat for seven minutes. Add the crumbled tempeh, garlic powder, cumin, salt and turmeric. Cook over medium heat for about five minutes, stirring frequently.
3. Add the spinach, cover the pot with a lid, reduce the heat to simmer and steam for a few minutes or until the kale is tender.
4. Makes four large portions.

Serving Suggestion: Serve the Tempeh Scramble with Spinach and Carrots with cup of coffee.

Variation Tip: Use tofu or chicken as a substitute of tempeh.

Nutritional Information per Serving:
Calories: 249 | **Fat:** 16.2g | **Sodium:** 632mg | **Carbs:** 13.9g | **Fiber:** 1.9g | **Sugar:** 2.2g | **Protein:** 16.9g

Overnight Oats

Prep time: 15 minutes
Cook time: 00 minutes
Serves: 2

Ingredients:

- 1 cup rolled oats
- 1 cup almond milk
- 2 tablespoons flax seeds
- 4 tablespoons pecans
- 1 tablespoon honey
- 2 teaspoons vanilla extract

Preparation:

1. Combine all the ingredients in a glass jar. Mix well, cover and refrigerate overnight.
2. Take it out of the fridge the next morning, stock up on your favorite fresh fruit and enjoy!

Serving Suggestion: Serve Overnight Oats with any kind of one fruit.

Variation Tip: Use any kind of healthy milk.

Nutritional Information per Serving:
Calories: 572 | **Fat:** 39.1g | **Sodium:** 23mg | **Carbs:** 47.1g | **Fiber:** 10.7g | **Sugar:** 11.4g | **Protein:** 11.8g

Kale Mozzarella Wrap

Prep time: 15 minutes
Cook time: 15 minutes
Serves: 2

Ingredients:

- 2 (7-inch) corn tortilla
- ½ cup sliced mushrooms
- ½ teaspoon black pepper
- 4 cups fresh kale
- 2 large egg, plus 1 egg white, lightly whisked
- 4 tablespoons crumbled mozzarella cheese
- 2 tablespoons sun-dried tomatoes, chopped

Preparation:

1. Place the tortilla on a microwaveable plate and heat on high for one minute.
2. Brush a small pot with cooking spray, then heat over medium heat. Sauté mushrooms and pepper for two minutes.
3. Add the kale and sauté for a minute or two, or until just tender.
4. Add the eggs and cook, stirring frequently, for about two minutes until ready.
5. Place the scrambled eggs in the center of the tortilla, then top with the crumbled mozzarella and sundried tomatoes. To wrap, fold one end and then both sides. Serve immediately or wrap in aluminium foil and take away.

Serving Suggestion: Serve Kale Mozzarella Wrap with sour cream and salsa.

Variation Tip: Use any kind of healthy tortillas.

Nutritional Information per Serving:
Calories: 245 | **Fat:** 12g | **Sodium:** 810mg | **Carbs:** 16.6g | **Fiber:** 3.3g | **Sugar:** 1.5g | **Protein:** 20.1g

Feta Egg Muffins

Prep time: 10 minutes
Cook time: 30 minutes
Serves: 6

Ingredients:

For the sausage:

- ½ tablespoon coconut oil
- ¼ onion, finely chopped
- ½ teaspoon garlic powder
- ¼ pound ground chicken
- ½ teaspoon dried thyme, crumbled
- ½ teaspoon cumin seeds
- ½ teaspoon dried basil
- ¼ teaspoon ground black pepper
- ½ teaspoon dried parsley
- ¼ teaspoon sea salt

For the muffins:

- 1 cup cauliflower, finely chopped
- ½ cup shredded feta cheese
- 1/8 cup sun-dried tomatoes (soaked in oil), finely chopped
- ½ teaspoon dried basil
- 1/8 teaspoon dried oregano
- ¼ teaspoon onion powder
- ¼ teaspoon sea salt
- 4 large eggs
- ½ tablespoon chives

Preparation:

1. Preheat the oven to 350°. Butter a 6-cup muffin pan.
2. In a medium skillet over medium heat, sauté onion and garlic for five minutes, or until onion is golden and tender. Remove from the pan and let cool for ten minutes.
3. In a medium bowl, combine the chicken and onion mixture. Add the rest of the sausage ingredients and mix well with your hands.
4. Shape the patties by hand to the desired width and thickness (3 inches wide and 1/2 inch to 3/4-inch-thick works well). Cook in the skillet over medium heat for eight minutes or until a thermometer in the middle reads 165° and the meat is no longer pink. Let cool, then chop the sausage and crumble into bite-sized pieces.
5. In a large bowl, combine the cauliflower, sausage, cheese, tomatoes, basil, oregano, onion powder and salt together.

6. Beat eggs in a medium bowl. Add to cauliflower mixture and mix well. Distribute the batter evenly over the muffin cups and sprinkle with chives.

7. Bake for 30 minutes or until a wooden toothpick inserted in the center of a muffin comes out clean.

Serving Suggestion: Serve the Feta Egg Muffins with ketchup.

Variation Tip: Add sweet corn to the muffins.

Nutritional Information per Serving:
Calories: 142 | **Fat:** 9.8g | **Sodium:** 209mg | **Carbs:** 2.6g | **Fiber:** 0.7g | **Sugar:** 0.9g | **Protein:** 12.3g

Frittata

Prep time: 15 minutes
Cook time: 15 minutes
Serves: 16

Ingredients:

- 2 tablespoon avocado oil
- 4 cups cherry tomatoes, halved
- 2 cups black beans
- 16 eggs
- 2 tablespoon fresh basil leaves, chopped (I used purple basil)
- Salt and pepper
- 2 ounces feta cheese, cubed

Preparation:

1. Pour the avocado oil into a small saucepan and add the tomatoes and beans. Sprinkle with a little salt and pepper and sauté for five minutes over medium heat. Lower the heat to low for two minutes.
2. In a small bowl, whisk together the eggs, basil, a little salt and pepper.
3. Slowly pour the egg mixture into the pan along with the tomatoes and beans. Add the cheese and stir a little. Cover and cook for 15 to 20 minutes or until the frittata is slightly puffed and cooked through on top.
4. Place the frittata on a large plate, let cool for a few minutes, cut into 16 wedges and serve hot.

Serving Suggestion: Serve the Frittata with salsa.

Variation Tip: Add broccoli to the Frittata.

Nutritional Information per Serving:
Calories: 186 | **Fat:** 7.8g | **Sodium:** 108mg | **Carbs:** 16.5g | **Fiber:** 4.2g | **Sugar:** 2g | **Protein:** 13.2g

Baked Eggs and Zoodles

Prep time: 15 minutes
Cook time: 15 minutes
Serves: 4

Ingredients:

- 6 zucchinis, spiralizer into noodles
- 4 tablespoons coconut oil
- Kosher salt and freshly ground black pepper
- 8 large eggs
- paprika, for garnishing
- Fresh cilantro, for garnishing
- 4 avocados, halved and thinly sliced

Preparation:

1. Preheat the oven to 350° F. Lightly grease a baking sheet with non-stick spray.
2. Combine zucchini noodles and coconut oil in a large bowl. Season with salt and pepper. Divide into four equal portions, place on a baking sheet and fit together.
3. Gently crack an egg in the middle of each nest. Bake until eggs are set, nine to 11 minutes.
4. Season with salt and pepper, garnish with paprika and basil flakes. Serve with avocado slices.

Serving Suggestion: Serve the Baked Eggs and Zoodles with sour cream and salsa.

Variation Tip: Add squash in case zucchini is not available.

Nutritional Information per Serving:
Calories: 721 | **Fat:** 63.1g | **Sodium:** 182mg | **Carbs:** 28g | **Fiber:** 15.8g | **Sugar:** 6.9g | **Protein:** 20.1g

Tortilla with Zucchini

Prep time: 15 minutes
Cook time: 15 minutes
Serves: 2

Ingredients:

- 2 sweet potato
- 4 tablespoons olive oil
- 2 onions, thinly sliced
- 1 zucchini, thinly sliced
- Kosher salt and freshly ground black pepper
- 6 large eggs
- 4 tablespoons grated Asiago cheese

Preparation:

1. Preheat the oven to 400° F.
2. In a medium saucepan, cover the sweet potato with at least 2.5 cm of water and bring to a boil over medium heat. Cook until sweet potato is tender with a fork, 22-25 minutes.
3. Drain the sweet potatoes, cut them into thin slices and keep them.
4. Heat the olive oil in a small ovenproof skillet over medium heat. Add the onion and zucchini and season with salt and pepper. Fry until tender, about four minutes.
5. Add the sweet potato wedges and sauté until all the vegetables are lightly brown, five to seven minutes. Distribute the vegetables in an even layer at the bottom of the pot. Remove the pan from the fire.
6. Beat eggs in medium bowl and pour over vegetables. Cover the eggs with the cheese.
7. Transfer the dish to the oven and bake until the eggs are cooked through and the potato and zucchini slices are golden on top, 12 to 15 minutes.

Serving Suggestion: Serve the Tortilla with Zucchini with salad.

Variation Tip: Add potatoes as a substitute of sweet potato.

Nutritional Information per Serving:
Calories: 682 | **Fat:** 43.1g | **Sodium:** 248mg | **Carbs:** 51.8g | **Fiber:** 7.5g | **Sugar:** 9.4g | **Protein:** 25.8g

Lime Poppy Seed Muffins

Prep time: 05 minutes
Cook time: 15 minutes
Serves: 4

Ingredients:

Dry ingredients

- ¾ cups almond flour
- ¾ teaspoon baking powder
- ¼ teaspoon baking soda
- 1/8 teaspoon salt
- 1 teaspoon poppy seeds

Wet ingredients

- Zest from 1 lime (about 1 tablespoon)
- ¼ cup maple syrup
- 1 egg
- ¼ cup plain Greek yogurt
- 1 tablespoon freshly squeezed lime juice
- 1/8 cup melted coconut oil

Preparation:

1. Preheat the oven to 400° F. Line a 12-muffin pan with four muffin cups and spray the insides of the cups with non-stick cooking spray. Don't stop spraying them!
2. In a medium bowl, whisk together almond flour, baking powder, baking powder, salt and poppy seeds. Put aside.
3. In a separate large bowl, add the lemon zest, maple syrup, eggs, yogurt and lime juice. Beat until smooth and well-mixed.
4. Gently stir in the dry ingredients until just combined, then add the cooled melted coconut
5. Distribute the batter evenly among four prepared muffin cups. Bake for 11-15 minutes or until tester comes out clean.

Serving Suggestion: Serve the Muffins with juice.

Variation Tip: Use black sesame seeds if poppy seed not available.

Nutritional Information per Serving:
Calories: 194 | **Fat:** 6.9g | **Sodium:** 175mg | **Carbs:** 29.1g | **Fiber:** 2.2g | **Sugar:** 14.8g | **Protein:** 4.7g

Egg and Veggie Breakfast Bowl

Prep time: 10 minutes
Cook time: 25 minutes
Serves: 2

Ingredients:

- ½ pound Brussels sprouts
- ½ pound potatoes
- ¾ tablespoon coconut oil
- 1 cup kale
- 2 eggs
- 2 tablespoons hot sauce
- 1½ tablespoons Sherry vinegar

Preparation:

1. Preheat the oven to 400° F. Line a baking sheet with parchment paper.
2. Cut the Brussels sprouts in half. Dice the potatoes.
3. Divide the Brussels sprouts and potatoes on the baking sheet. Pour coconut oil evenly over the vegetables. Season with salt and pepper.
4. Toast in the oven until golden brown and tender, 17 to 20 minutes.
5. In a small bowl, whisk the hot sauce with the coconut oil and Sherry vinegar.
6. Poach or fry the eggs.
7. To serve, divide the Brussels sprouts and potatoes among four bowls. Top each with ½ cup kale and one egg. Drizzle each bowl with two teaspoons of the harissa vinaigrette.

Serving Suggestion: Serve the Egg and Veggie Breakfast Bowl with juice.

Variation Tip: Add more vegetables you like.

Nutritional Information per Serving:
Calories: 441 | **Fat:** 25.1g | **Sodium:** 193mg | **Carbs:** 45.7g | **Fiber:** 9.5g | **Sugar:** 5.6g | **Protein:** 11.9g

Green Shakshuka

Prep time: 20 minutes
Cook time: 25 minutes
Serves: 2

Ingredients:

- 1 tablespoon olive oil
- 1 small onion, minced
- 1 garlic clove, minced
- 1 jalapeño, seeded and minced
- ½ pound kale
- ½ teaspoon dried cumin
- 2 teaspoons coriander
- Salt and freshly ground black pepper
- 1 tablespoons harissa
- ¼ cup vegetable broth
- 4 large eggs
- Chopped fresh parsley, as needed for serving
- Chopped fresh cilantro, as needed for serving
- Red-pepper flakes, as needed for serving

Preparation:

1. Preheat the oven to 350° F.
2. In a large ovenproof skillet, heat olive oil over medium heat. Add onion and sauté until tender, four to five minutes. Add the garlic and jalapeño and sauté one more minute until fragrant.
3. Add kale and cook until completely tender, four to five minutes, or until heated through, if thawed, one to two minutes.
4. Season with cumin, coriander, salt, pepper and harissa. Cook for about one minute until fragrant.
5. Pour the mixture into the bowl of a food processor or blender and blend until thick. Add the broth and puree until thick and smooth.
6. Clean the pan and grease it with non-stick cooking spray. Pour the kale mixture into the pot and use a wooden spoon to make eight round hollows.
7. Carefully break the eggs into the notches. Transfer the pot to the oven and cook until the egg whites are completely set but the yolks are still lightly stirred, 20 to 25 minutes.
8. Sprinkle the shakshuka with parsley, cilantro and paprika flakes of your choice. Use immediately.

Serving Suggestion: Serve the Green Shakshuka with warm crusty bread or pita.

Variation Tip: Add spinach in green shakshuka.

Nutritional Information per Serving:
Calories: 386 | **Fat:** 23.1g | **Sodium:** 674mg | **Carbs:** 26g | **Fiber:** 5g | **Sugar:** 9.8g | **Protein:** 18g

Poultry Recipes

Beans and Chicken Stir Fry

Prep time: 05 minutes
Cook time: 30 minutes
Serves: 6

Ingredients:

- 2 teaspoon coconut oil
- 4 cups fresh green beans trimmed and halved
- 2 tablespoons fresh ginger thinly sliced
- 6 Scallions sliced
- 4 cloves fresh garlic diced
- 6 boneless, skinless, chicken breast sliced thin
- 4 tablespoons coconut aminos
- 4 tablespoons apple cider vinegar
- 2 teaspoons white sesame seed

Preparation:

1. Heat a large skillet over medium heat, add one teaspoon of coconut oil and add the green beans, garlic, ginger, Scallions and one tablespoon of coconut aminos. Cook four to five minutes, stirring constantly.
2. Remove the green bean mixture from the pan and add one teaspoon of coconut oil to start cooking the chicken. Place the chicken in the pan to cover the entire bottom of the pan, leave the chicken intact for three to four minutes to brown on one side.
3. Then stir the chicken and cook for another two to three minutes. When the chicken is almost completely cooked, return the bean mixture to the pan along with the coconut aminos, vinegar and coconut oil.
4. Mix and cook for another two minutes until the chicken is cooked through.
5. Serve the chicken and green beans. Sprinkle white sesame seeds.

Serving Suggestion: Serve the Beans and Chicken Stir Fry with your brown rice.

Variation Tip: Use turkey as a substitute of chicken.

Nutritional Information per Serving:
Calories: 386 | **Fat:** 15.1g | **Sodium:** 634mg | **Carbs:** 46g | **Fiber:** 7g | **Sugar:** 4.2g | **Protein:** 8.5g

Mushroom and Chicken

Prep time: 05 minutes
Cook time: 35 minutes
Serves: 4

Ingredients:

- 15 ounces boneless, skinless, chicken breast (about 2 large breast)
- ¼ teaspoon black pepper
- ¼ teaspoon garlic powder
- ½ tablespoon extra-virgin olive oil
- 1½ cups White Mushrooms sliced, (about 120 grams)
- 2 cups yellow onion diced,
- 2 cloves fresh garlic diced,
- 1¼ cups water
- 1 cup orzo
- Dash tsp Salt
- ¼ teaspoon black pepper
- ¼ teaspoon garlic powder
- 1½ cups spinach torn
- ¼ cup Dubliner Cheese or any white cheddar cheese, freshly shredded

Preparation:

1. Heat a large, deep skillet over medium heat. While waiting for the pan to heat, season the chicken with pepper and garlic powder. Once the pan is hot, add extra virgin olive oil to the pan.
2. Immediately put the chicken in the pan, leave it there for two minutes, then turn it over and cook for another two minutes.
3. Both sides should start to brown, but the center will still look raw if it isn't golden. Give each side an extra min. Reduce the heat to low and cover the chicken with a lid. Cook for about seven minutes, then flip and cover for another seven minutes.
4. After seven minutes covered on each side, the chicken should be cooked. However, it will depend on the size of the chicken breast.
5. It is always best to check the internal temperature of the chicken before serving.
6. Once the chicken is cooked, remove it from the pan and leave the juice in the pan.
7. Over medium heat, add the mushrooms, chopped onion and garlic with the juice in the pan. Chicken juice adds a lot of flavor to this dish. Cook the mushrooms and onions, stirring regularly, for about five minutes, until they soften and become fragrant.
8. After five minutes, add water and orzo to the pot. Season with additional salt, pepper and garlic salt. Bring the water to a boil and cook until most of the water has evaporated/soaked

in the orzo. Stir frequently to prevent the orzo from burning at the bottom of the pot. It usually takes eight to ten minutes to cook the orzo. At this point, the orzo should be done.

9. While the orzo is cooking, we put a fork and a knife to chop the chicken.

10. Add the spinach, pulled chicken and cheese to the pan. Cook for another two minutes, until the spinach has collapsed and the cheese is incorporated into the orzo.

Serving Suggestion: Serve the Mushroom and Chicken with warm crusty bread or pita.

Variation Tip: Add kale as an alternative to spinach.

Nutritional Information Per Serving:
Calories: 500 | **Fat:** 6.7g | **Sodium:** 106mg | **Carbs:** 69.8g | **Fiber:** 4.5g | **Sugar:** 6.3g | **Protein:** 39g

Baked Ranch Chicken

Prep time: 10 minutes
Cook time: 30 minutes
Serves: 4

Ingredients:

- 26 ounce boneless skinless chicken breasts about 1.5 pounds
- ½ teaspoon salt
- ½ teaspoon pepper
- 1-ounce packet ranch seasoning
- 6 tablespoon sour cream
- ½ cup breadcrumbs
- 6 tablespoon shredded feta cheese
- 1/8 cup grated goat cheese
- 1 tablespoon olive oil

Preparation:

1. Using a meat mallet or rolling pin, pound chicken breasts until each is ¼ inch thick. This allows the chicken to cook quickly and evenly. Sprinkle both sides with salt and pepper, then set aside.
2. In a medium bowl, combine sour cream and two tablespoon of the ranch seasoning package.
3. Add the chicken breasts to the sour cream mixture and toss with tongs or your hands until the chicken is completely coated.
4. Cover the chicken and let it marinate for at least an hour. If you can prepare this step in the morning or evening to marinate longer, so much better.
5. Preheat the oven to 425°.
6. In a medium bowl, combine remaining ranch dressing mix, breadcrumbs, feta and grated goat cheese.
7. Dip the marinated chicken breasts in the bread mixture and place them in a pan or casserole dish coated with olive oil.
8. Spread the rest of the breadcrumbs mixture over the chicken breast.
9. Bake for 25 to 30 minutes or until the chicken is cooked through. The internal temperature of the chicken should be 165° when fully cooked.
10. Serve hot.

Serving Suggestion: Serve the Baked Ranch Chicken with salad, rice or vegetables.

Variation Tip: Use panko bread crumbs if you go for low carb.

Nutritional Information per Serving:
Calories: 251 | **Fat:** 11g | **Sodium:** 574mg | **Carbs:** 10g | **Fiber:** 5g | **Sugar:** 2g | **Protein:** 29g

Turkey Burgers with Savory Warm Relish

Prep time: 20 minutes
Cook time: 25 minutes
Serves: 2

Ingredients:

- Ground turkey (¼ pound patties, 93% lean) seasoned with a little salt & pepper
- 1 small onion
- ½ red bell pepper thinly sliced
- 2 cups red cabbage shredded
- 1 tablespoon coconut oil
- ¼ cup balsamic vinegar
- ¼ tablespoon garlic salt
- 2 large leaves of lettuce (romaine, red leaf, or green leaf)

Preparation:

1. Wash and dry the lettuce leaves.
2. In a large skillet, sauté the onion, bell pepper and red cabbage with coconut oil until tender.
3. Add the garlic salt and balsamic vinegar and simmer until the vinegar and vegetables are shiny and caramelized. Stir frequently.
4. Keep this spice warm.
5. Grill or fry turkey burgers until just cooked through. Usually four minutes per side on a hot grill, but a little longer if using the frozen grill.
6. Now place a turkey burger at the end of the stem of the lettuce leaf and cover with a generous dollop of hot spices.

Serving Suggestion: Serve the Turkey Burger with mayonnaise.

Variation Tip: If you like chicken use ground chicken.

Nutritional Information per Serving:
Calories: 258 | **Fat:** 13g | **Sodium:** 474mg | **Carbs:** 10g | **Fiber:** 3g | **Sugar:** 9.8g | **Protein:** 23g

Pesto Chicken and Veggies

Prep time: 10 minutes
Cook time: 20 minutes
Serves: 2

Ingredients:

- 2 tablespoon coconut oil
- ½ pound chicken thighs boneless and skinless, sliced into strips
- 1/6 cup sun-dried tomatoes drained of oil, chopped
- ½ pound asparagus ends trimmed, cut in half, if large
- 1/8 cup basil pesto
- ½ cup cherry tomatoes, yellow and red, halved

Preparation:

1. Heat a large skillet over medium heat, add one tablespoon of coconut oil, add the sliced chicken thighs, generously season the chicken with salt, add half of the chopped sundried tomatoes and cook over medium heat for five to ten minutes, turning a few times until chicken is cooked through. Take out the chicken and let it dry out of the pan, leave the oil on.
2. The asparagus (cut ends), generously season with salt, add the remaining half of the sun-dried tomatoes and cook over medium heat for five to ten minutes until the asparagus is cooked through. Remove the asparagus to a serving platter.
3. Add the chicken to the pan, add the pesto, stir over medium heat until the chicken is heated through, one to two minutes. Remove from the stove. Add the cherry tomatoes cut in half, mix with the pesto and the chicken. Place the chicken and tomatoes with the asparagus on the plate.

Serving Suggestion: Serve Pesto Chicken and Veggies with salad.

Variation Tip: Add green beans as a substitute with asparagus.

Nutritional Information per Serving:
Calories: 423 | **Fat:** 32g | **Sodium:** 261mg | **Carbs:** 12g | **Fiber:** 4g | **Sugar:** 7g | **Protein:** 23g

Easy Turkey Salad

Prep time: 05 minutes
Cook time: 25 minutes
Serves: 12

Ingredients:

- 4 pounds boneless skinless turkey breasts, cooked and shredded
- 3 cups halved red grapes
- 1 cup chopped walnuts
- 1 cup diced green onions
- 1 cup plain Greek yogurt
- 1 cup mayonnaise
- ½ cup Dijon mustard
- ¼ teaspoon dried sage
- 1 teaspoon smoked paprika
- ½ teaspoon garlic powder
- 2 tablespoons of fresh lemon juice
- Salt & pepper to taste

Preparation:

1. In a large bowl, add the grated turkey, red grapes, walnuts and green onions.
2. In a small bowl, add the yogurt, mayonnaise, Dijon mustard, sage, smoked paprika powder, garlic powder, lemon juice, salt and pepper. Beat together.
3. Pour the liquid mixture into the chicken bowl.
4. Mix everything until it is completely combined.
5. Serve on a slice of bread or in a cup of salad.

Serving Suggestion: Serve the Turkey Salad with bread.

Variation Tip: Use pecans as a substitute of walnuts.

Nutritional Information per Serving:
Calories: 186 | **Fat:** 10g | **Sodium:** 157mg | **Carbs:** 7g | **Fiber:** 1g | **Sugar:** 4g | **Protein:** 18g

Chipotle Chicken Bowl

Prep time: 25 minutes
Cook time: 15 minutes
Serves: 2

Ingredients:

- ½ pound boneless, skinless chicken breasts
- 2 bay leaves
- Peppercorns
- ½ pouch cooked quinoa
- 4 cups Romaine lettuce, chopped (about 2 hearts of Romaine)
- 1 cups tomato salsa
- Small handful fresh cilantro, chopped
- Fresh lemon, squeezed

Preparation:

1. Place the chicken in a saucepan large enough to hold and fill it with enough water (or chicken broth) to cover the chicken by about one to two inches.
2. Add two bay leaves, sprigs of fresh parsley and whole peppercorns to flavor the cooking liquid to taste, then bring to a boil over high heat.
3. When the water boils, cover the pot with a lid and reduce the heat to low. Simmer the chicken for ten to 15 minutes, or until the inside temperature of the thickest part of the breast is 165° F.
4. Use tongs to remove the chicken and place it on a plate. When it is cold enough to handle, crush it and set it aside.
5. cook quinoa according to the directions on the package.
6. Assemble each bowl by adding two cups of romaine lettuce, ½ cup of quinoa, three ounces of chicken (¼ of the chicken), ½ cup of salsa and garnish with fresh cilantro and a lemon wedge.

Serving Suggestion: Serve the Chipotle Chicken Bowl with salad.

Variation Tip: Add rice if you don't like quinoa.

Nutritional Information per Serving:
Calories: 246 | **Fat:** 5g | **Sodium:** 664mg | **Carbs:** 29g | **Fiber:** 5g | **Sugar:** 4g | **Protein:** 28g

Turkey Parmesan Zucchini Boats

Prep time: 10 minutes
Cook time: 45 minutes
Serves: 2

Ingredients:

- 2 medium zucchinis
- ½ pound ground turkey
- 1/8 teaspoon salt
- 1/8 teaspoon ground black pepper
- 1 garlic clove minced
- ½ cup pasta sauce
- 1/8 cup grated parmesan cheese
- ¼ cup shredded mozzarella cheese
- Optional: Sliced fresh basil for topping

Preparation:

1. Preheat oven to 400° F. Spray 9x13-inch pan with cooking spray.
2. Place a large non-stick skillet over medium-high heat. Add the turkey. Add salt and pepper. Cook, eight to ten minutes, until the chicken is cooked through. Stir occasionally and break the chicken into small pieces.
3. Reduce the heat to a minimum. Add the garlic to the turkey. Cook for one minute, stirring frequently. Add the pasta sauce. Cook for three minutes, stirring occasionally.
4. While the turkey cooks, cut the zucchini in half lengthwise. Use a spoon to scoop out the seeds and center of each zucchini half, leaving a ¼-inch-thick zucchini pan.
5. Place the zucchini in a baking dish with the cut surface facing up.
6. Pour the turkey mixture into the zucchini glasses. Use the back of the spoon to press the mixture into the zucchini.
7. Sprinkle the zucchini evenly with Parmesan, then mozzarella.
8. Cover the baking dish with foil. Bake for 35 minutes.
9. Sprinkle with fresh basil and serve.

Serving Suggestion: Serve Turkey Parmesan Zucchini Boats with crusty bread or pita.

Variation Tip: Use chicken as a substitute of turkey.

Nutritional Information per Serving:
Calories: 332 | **Fat:** 17.8g | **Sodium:** 674mg | **Carbs:** 13.3g | **Fiber:** 2g | **Sugar:** 9.8g | **Protein:** 38g

Roasted Garlic & Herb Chicken and Veggies

Prep time: 10 minutes
Cook time: 20 minutes
Serves: 12

Ingredients:

- 3 pounds boneless skinless chicken breasts cut into 1-inch pieces
- 4 cups broccoli florets
- 2 large zucchinis cut 1 into inch pieces
- 2 medium onion cut into 1-inch pieces
- 2 bells pepper any color, cut into 1-inch pieces
- 2 cup grape tomatoes cut into 1-inch pieces

For the Garlic & Herb marinade:

- 1/2 cup olive oil
- 8 cloves garlic crushed or finely chopped,
- 4 tablespoons Gourmet Garden lightly dried parsley or chive or basil
- 4 tablespoons Gourmet Garden lightly dried cilantro
- 2 teaspoon chili pepper flakes
- Salt and freshly ground black pepper
- 2 teaspoon ginger optional
- Juice of 1 lime

Preparation:

1. Preheat the oven to 450° F.
2. In a medium bowl, combine the garlic, herbs, salt and pepper, and lemon juice.
3. Place the chicken and vegetables in a pan and drizzle with the garlic and herb mixture. Toss with your hands until all the chicken and vegetables are coated.
4. Bake for 20 to 22 minutes or until chicken and vegetables are cooked through.
5. Serve fresh.

Serving Suggestion: Serve the Roasted Garlic & Herb Chicken and Veggies with hot rice or quinoa.

Variation Tip: Use chicken as a substitute of turkey.

Nutritional Information per Serving:
Calories: 386 | **Fat:** 23.1g | **Sodium:** 674mg | **Carbs:** 26g | **Fiber:** 5g | **Sugar:** 9.8g | **Protein:** 18g

Lemon Basil Chicken

Prep time: 15 minutes
Cook time: 15 minutes
Serves: 2

Ingredients:

- ½ tablespoon coconut oil
- ¼ large yellow onion finely chopped
- 2 cloves garlic minced
- ¾ pounds boneless skinless chicken breasts, cut into 3/4-inch pieces
- 1 tablespoon coconut aminos
- 1/8 teaspoon ground black pepper
- 2½ cups loosely packed baby kale
- ½ tablespoon lemon zest
- 1 tablespoon freshly squeezed lemon juice
- 2 cup fresh basil leaves
- Kosher salt and pepper to taste

Preparation:

1. In a large skillet, heat coconut oil over medium heat. When hot, add onion and cook, stirring frequently, until just tender, about four minutes. Add the garlic and cook until fragrant, another 30 seconds.
2. Add the chicken, increase the heat to medium and cook for three minutes, browning all sides. Add coconut, aminos and black pepper. Cook until chicken is cooked through, about three minutes more.
3. Add the kale a few handfuls at a time while allowing the heat of the pan to wilt. Add the lemon zest, lemon juice and basil. Cook and stir until basil is tender, about one minute more. Season to taste and add salt or pepper to taste. Serve hot with rice to taste.

Serving Suggestion: Serve the Lemon Basil Chicken with rice.

Variation Tip: Add spinach as a substitute of kale.

Nutritional Information per Serving:
Calories: 349 | **Fat:** 8g | **Sodium:** 534mg | **Carbs:** 29g | **Fiber:** 5g | **Sugar:** 3g | **Protein:** 40g

Fish and Seafood Recipes

Moroccan Salmon

Prep time: 05 minutes
Cook time: 15 minutes
Serves: 4

Ingredients:

- 4 (thick) salmon filets 4-6 ounces each
- 1 teaspoon nutmeg
- 1 teaspoon cumin
- 1 teaspoon salt
- 1½ teaspoons honey
- Pinch cayenne or smoked paprika
- 2 tablespoons olive oil for searing
- Garnish orange zest

Preparation:

1. Preheat oven to 350° F.
2. Combine nutmeg, cumin, salt, honey and cayenne pepper in a small bowl.
3. Sprinkle both sides of the salmon.
4. Heat the olive oil in a pan (cast iron) over medium heat. Sear the salmon on both sides for two minutes per side, then place in a hot oven for five minutes or until cooked through.
5. Garnish with orange zest.

Serving Suggestion: Serve the Moroccan Salmon with rice.

Variation Tip: Use sugar as a substitute of honey.

Nutritional Information per Serving:
Calories: 297 | **Fat:** 15.3g | **Sodium:** 716.1mg | **Carbs:** 3.2g | **Fiber:** 0.5g | **Sugar:** 1.7g | **Protein:** 38.2g

Simple Salmon Chowder

Prep time: 10 minutes
Cook time: 25 minutes
Serves: 12

Ingredients:

- 4 leeks, sliced
- 2 small fennel bulbs
- 2 cup celery, sliced
- 8 garlic cloves, rough chopped
- 2 teaspoon fennel seeds (optional)
- 1 teaspoon thyme (dry, or 2 teaspoons fresh)
- 1 teaspoon smoked paprika
- ¼ cup white wine
- 6 cups chicken broth
- 1½ pounds baby potatoes, thinly sliced
- 2 teaspoon salt
- 2 bay leaf
- 2 pounds salmon, skinless.
- 4 cups coconut milk
- Garnish: Fennel fronds, lemon wedges, fresh dill or tarragon

Preparation:

1. Heat the oil over medium heat and sauté the leek, fennel and celery for five to six minutes until fragrant. Add the garlic, fennel seeds and thyme and sauté for two more minutes. Add the smoked paprika powder.
2. Add the white wine and cook for about one to two minutes. Add the broth, salt, thyme and bay leaf and simmer over high heat. Add the potatoes and stir. Bring to a boil, cover and cook over medium heat until tender, about eight to ten minutes (check after seven minutes, be careful not to cook for too long). While cooking, prepare the salmon.
3. Cut the salmon into 2-inch pieces, sprinkle salt lightly.
4. When the potatoes are tender, add the milk and simmer (do not boil) and add the salmon in the soup for about two minutes. Put out the fire. The fish will continue to cook. Simmering the soup longer can cause it to curdle slightly. (Don't worry, it's still edible, but not quite as nice.) Use a fork to cut the fish into bite-sized pieces.
5. Season to taste, and serve immediately.
6. Garnish with fennel leaves, lemon wedges, fresh dill or tarragon.

Serving Suggestion: Serve Salmon Chowder with salad.

Variation Tip: Substitute potatoes with cauliflower.

Nutritional Information per Serving:
Calories: 285 | **Fat:** 12.1g | **Sodium:** 700mg | **Carbs:** 20.7g | **Fiber:** 3.5g | **Sugar:** 8.1g | **Protein:** 24.1g

Sweet and Sour Tuna

Prep time: 05 minutes
Cook time: 30 minutes
Serves: 2

Ingredients:

- 10 ounces tuna
- 1 tablespoon coconut oil
- 1 tablespoon Mirin
- 1 tablespoon maple syrup
- 2 tablespoon soy sauce
- 1 teaspoon chili garlic sauce
- 1 tablespoon sweet & sour sauce
- 1 teaspoon sesame seed
- 2 stalk scallions sliced, (6 grams)
- ½ cup quinoa
- 2 head Baby Bok Choy, washed and separated

Preparation:

1. Boil the quinoa: Bring water to a boil. Add the quinoa, cover with a lid and lower the heat. Cook over low heat for 20 minutes then remove from heat. Keep it covered for another ten minutes.
2. While the quinoa is cooking, prepare the tuna.
3. In a small bowl, combine the mirin, maple syrup, low sodium soy sauce, sweet & sour sauce and chili garlic sauce.
4. Preheat a medium sized pan with a lid over medium heat, add coconut oil to the pan. Place the tuna skin side down in the pan. Spread the sweet & sour sauce mixture. Simmer for three minutes. Then cover with the lid for another three to four minutes.
5. While the tuna cooks, heat a large pan on medium heat. Place the Bok Choi in the pan and cook for about one minute. Then pour the additional soy sauce over it. Cook for about five minutes, turning every 45 seconds to avoid scorching.
6. Dish: First put the rice in a bowl, then garnish with Bok Choy and tuna. Spread the rest of the sweet & sour mixture over the tuna. Sprinkle with sesame seeds and chives.

Serving Suggestion: Serve the Sweet and Sour Tuna with rice or quinoa.

Variation Tip: Add honey as a substitute of maple syrup.

Nutritional Information per Serving:
Calories: 553 | **Fat:** 19.8g | **Sodium:** 1404mg | **Carbs:** 50.8g | **Fiber:** 3.6g | **Sugar:** 14g | **Protein:** 36.5g

Baked Cod with Tomatoes & Basil

Prep time: 10 minutes
Cook time: 15 minutes
Serves: 8

Ingredients:

- 6 tablespoons coconut oil
- 4 cups cherry or grape tomatoes
- 3 pounds cod fillets
- Salt, pepper and chili flakes to taste
- 2 lemon – zest (set aside) and slices
- 6 garlic cloves rough chopped
- 1/2 cup basil leaves torn

Preparation:

1. Preheat the oven at 400° F.
2. Pour coconut oil into a 9x13-inch baking dish. Distribute the garlic cloves. Add the tomatoes and lemon wedges and mix. put aside.
3. Dry the fish and place it in the baking dish, turning it over with tongs to brush each side of the fish with oil. Spread the tomato and garlic mixture and heat the fish – tomatoes on the sides, lemons below. Season generously with salt, pepper and chili flakes.
4. Bake for ten minutes. Shake the pan well, squeezing the tomatoes a little. Sprinkle lemon zest. Cook for another five minutes or until the fish is cooked to your liking.
5. When you are done, add the broken basil leaves and throw them in the hot tomatoes with tongs so that the basil collapses a bit. Then garnish each piece of fish with a wilted basil leaf.
6. Serve immediately!

Serving Suggestion: Serve the Baked Cod with rice or cauliflower rice.

Variation Tip: Add any kind of fish.

Nutritional Information per Serving:
Calories: 227 | **Fat:** 11.7g | **Sodium:** 373mg | **Carbs:** 4.5g | **Fiber:** 1.5g | **Sugar:** 2.5g | **Protein:** 26.2g

Zucchini Noodles and Lemon Shrimp

Prep time: 10 minutes
Cook time: 15 minutes
Serves: 6

Ingredients:

- 8 medium zucchini, noodled,
- 28 ounces shrimp, uncooked, fresh, peeled and deveined
- 2 lemons juiced
- 2 teaspoons black pepper
- 2 teaspoons garlic powder
- ½ teaspoon old bay seasoning
- 1 tablespoon unsalted butter
- ½ teaspoon salt
- 2 tablespoon Italian Parsley

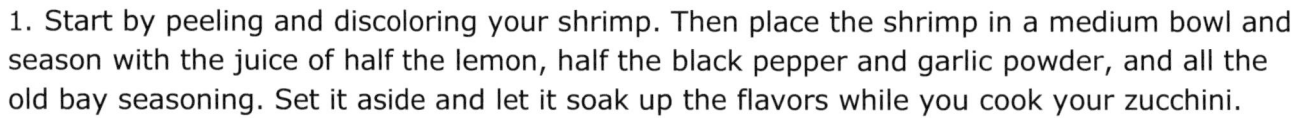

Preparation:

1. Start by peeling and discoloring your shrimp. Then place the shrimp in a medium bowl and season with the juice of half the lemon, half the black pepper and garlic powder, and all the old bay seasoning. Set it aside and let it soak up the flavors while you cook your zucchini.
2. Cut the zucchini into thin noodles using a cookie cutter. Then season the noodles with salt and the remaining half of the lemon.
3. Heat a large skillet over medium-low heat. Add the shrimp and juice to the pan. Spread the shrimp in an even layer. Cook for three minutes, then flip and fry on the other side for another two minutes.
4. Now add the zucchini noodles and the butter with the shrimp to the pan. Mix everything together and season with the other half of the pepper and garlic powder. Then cover with a lid and cook for five minutes, half removing the lid and stirring.
5. Serve with a pinch of fresh parsley and a lemon wedge.

Serving Suggestion: Serve the Zucchini Noodles and Lemon Shrimp with bread.

Variation Tip: Use squash as a substitute of zucchini.

Nutritional Information per Serving:
Calories: 201 | **Fat:** 3.3g | **Sodium:** 387mg | **Carbs:** 7.6g | **Fiber:** 2.5g | **Sugar:** 4.7g | **Protein:** 36.5g

Ceviche

Prep time: 25 minutes
Cook time: 30 minutes
Serves: 12

Ingredients:

- 1 onion, very thinly sliced
- 2-pound fresh fish – sea bass, red snapper, corvina, dorado, escolar, mahi-mahi, tilapia, or Hamachi – diced into ½ inch cubes.
- 6 garlic cloves very finely minced
- 3 teaspoon kosher salt, start with 1, add more to taste
- ½ teaspoon black pepper
- 1 cup fresh cilantro chopped
- 2 fresh serrano or jalapeño chili pepper seeded and very finely chopped
- 8 fresh lemon freshly squeezed
- 2 cups grape or cherry tomatoes, cut in half
- 2 cups diced cucumber
- 2 tablespoon coconut oil (optional)
- 2 semi-firm Avocado, diced, as garnish, optional

Preparation:

1. Finely chop the onion and salt it liberally and let it sit for 15 minutes, until it begins to release its liquid (this will remove the bitterness). Rinse well, squeeze to dry.
2. Place the fish, garlic, onion, salt, pepper, fresh jalapeño peppers and lemon juice in a shallow serving bowl, mix gently and marinate in the refrigerator for at least 30 minutes before serving.
3. Before serving, gently add the fresh cilantro, cucumber and tomato and a drizzle of coconut oil and mix gently.
4. Taste the salt and add more if necessary. If you're adding avocado, fold it over carefully after everything is mixed, being careful not to use an overly smooth one.

Serving Suggestion: Serve the Ceviche with chips.

Variation Tip: Add garlic powder if garlic is not available.

Nutritional Information per Serving:
Calories: 149 | **Fat:** 6.3g | **Sodium:** 637.1mg | **Carbs:** 9g | **Fiber:** 3.1g | **Sugar:** 3.2g | **Protein:** 15.5g

Spicy Shrimp and Sautéed Kale

Prep time: 05 minutes
Cook time: 10 minutes
Serves: 2

Ingredients:

- 1 tablespoon unsalted butter
- 6 cloves fresh garlic diced
- 1 jalapeno pepper diced
- 24 large shrimps uncooked, peeled and deveined
- 1 cup baby kale
- 1 teaspoon red pepper flake
- 1 teaspoon black pepper

Preparation:

1. Heat two medium pans over medium heat.
2. Once they are hot, add ¼ tablespoon of butter to each pan. Then add half the diced garlic and half the diced jalapeño to each pan and mix with the butter.
3. In a skillet, add the shrimp, add the melted butter and brown the shrimp on one side for about three minutes.
4. Put the kale in the other saucepan and mix with the melted butter. Add the red pepper flakes and continue to mix for about three minutes. The kale will start to wilt. Reduce the heat to low and let it sit while you work with the shrimp.
5. Stir in the shrimp, garlic and jalapeños. Then turn each shrimp on its opposite side. Cook for another two to three minutes or until cooked through.
6. While you wait for the shrimp to finish, place the sautéed kale on a plate. Season with a pinch of freshly ground black pepper.
7. Now that the shrimps are fully cooked, toss them to absorb the flavors of the pan.
8. Garnish the kale with the cooked shrimp and a few kale jalapeños and garlic that remain in the pan. Finally, decorate with a few black peppercorns, a pinch of red pepper flakes and finely scraped red onion.

Serving Suggestion: Serve the Spicy Shrimp and Sautéed Kale with noodles.

Variation Tip: Add spinach as a substitute of kale.

Nutritional Information per Serving:
Calories: 230 | **Fat:** 5.6g | **Sodium:** 625mg | **Carbs:** 11.9g | **Fiber:** 5.4g | **Sugar:** 2.8g | **Protein:** 30.3g

Quick and Easy Salmon Cakes

Prep time: 15 minutes
Cook time: 15 minutes
Serves: 4

Ingredients:

- 14 ounces, drained (or feel free to use leftover cooked salmon)
- 2 eggs
- 2 tablespoons mayo
- 2 teaspoons lemon juice
- 1 teaspoon garlic powder
- ½ cup toasted bread crumbs like plain panko (okay to use GF) or flour
- 4 scallions, sliced
- Generous pinch salt and pepper (about ⅛ teaspoon each – see notes)
- Olive oil for searing

Preparation:

1. Combine all ingredients in a medium bowl with a fork. Let stand five to ten minutes.
2. If the mixture seems too wet, add a little more breadcrumb (up to 1/3 cup total).
3. Divide the mixture into two large cakes by pressing down with your hands. If you like a crispy crust, dredge more panko (optional) and/or sesame seeds before browning.
4. Heat oil or butter (or a good mixture) in a pan over medium heat. Fry the salmon patties on each side for four to five minutes until golden brown and slightly puffed.
5. Serve with the quick cream sauce or simply with a salad.

Serving Suggestion: Serve the Salmon Cakes with salad.

Variation Tip: Try to use unseasoned panko or bread crumbs.

Nutritional Information per Serving:
Calories: 298 | **Fat:** 15g | **Sodium:** 584mg | **Carbs:** 4.2g | **Fiber:** 0.5g | **Sugar:** 0.9g | **Protein:** 36.5g

Roasted Mustard Seed White Fish

Prep time: 15 minutes
Cook time: 30 minutes
Serves: 4

Ingredients:

- 20 ounces potatoes, thinly sliced (⅛ inch thick)
- 2 large shallots, thinly sliced
- 2 tablespoons coconut oil
- Salt and pepper to taste
- 16 ounces Brussel Sprouts, thinly sliced
- Pinch caraway seeds (optional)
- 4- or 6-ounce filets of fish
- 8 teaspoons whole grain mustard
- 4 teaspoons olive oil

Preparation:

1. Preheat Oven at 450° F.
2. Cut the potatoes and shallots and mix with the oil, salt and pepper in a bowl. Place them in a single layer on a baking sheet lined with parchment paper (save the bowl) and bake for 20 minutes.
3. Slice the brussels sprouts and place them in the same oily container. Mix, add a pinch of caraway seeds and a little salt and pepper if you wish. Put aside.
4. Put the whole mustard and oil in a small bowl and season the fish with salt & pepper. Distribute the mustard mixture and place it over the fish.
5. After 20 minutes of cooking the potatoes, add the brussels sprouts and mix a little. Make room for the fish. Cook for another ten to 12 minutes, until the fish is cooked through.
6. Divide the hash browns and brussels sprouts between two bowls and top with the mustard glazed fish. Serve with optional sauerkraut.

Serving Suggestion: Serve the Roasted Mustard Seed White Fish with sauerkraut.

Variation Tip: Substitute fish with chicken breast or tofu.

Nutritional Information per Serving:
Calories: 318 | **Fat:** 12.8g | **Sodium:** 386mg | **Carbs:** 35.9g | **Fiber:** 7.5g | **Sugar:** 4.1g | **Protein:** 18.6g

Baked Salmon Recipe with Asparagus & Yogurt Dill Sauce

Prep time: 10 minutes
Cook time: 30 minutes
Serves: 2

Ingredients:

- ½ large bunch asparagus
- 2 salmon filets
- 1 tablespoon coconut oil
- Salt and pepper to taste
- lemon zest from one lemon (divided)

Yogurt Dill Sauce

- ¼ cup plain whole fat yogurt
- ½ tablespoon olive oil
- 1 garlic clove, finely minced
- Lemon zest (of ½ a lemon)
- 1/8 teaspoon salt
- 1/8 cup chopped dill
- 1/8 cup chopped parsley (optional)
- Squeeze of lemon to taste
- Cracked pepper to taste

Preparation:

1. Preheat oven at 375° F.
2. Cut off the hard ends of the asparagus and mix with a drizzle of coconut oil, salt and pepper. Place on a baking sheet lined with baking paper.
3. Place the salmon in the middle of the asparagus and drizzle with coconut oil, sprinkle with salt and pepper and sprinkle the salmon and asparagus with the zest of one lemon (save the remaining zest for the yogurt sauce).
4. Place in a preheated 375° F oven for 16-20 minutes, adjust the time according to the thickness of the salmon and grill the last few minutes as desired for medium sized cooked salmon. If you are cooking smaller pieces of salmon it may take less time, so check beforehand and remove if necessary to make the asparagus cook longer.
5. While the salmon is cooking, prepare the dill and yogurt sauce: Place all the ingredients in a small bowl and whisk with a fork. If desired, add a splash of lemon juice and ground pepper. The taste of the garlic will mellow when it becomes firm.
6. Divide the salmon and asparagus on plates, pour a little yogurt-dill sauce on top and garnish with a sprig of dill if you wish. Serve with a lemon wedge.

Serving Suggestion: Serve the Baked Salmon Recipe with Asparagus with yogurt dill sauce

Variation Tip: Use tuna as a substitute of salmon.

Nutritional Information per Serving:
Calories: 252 | **Fat:** 13.2g | **Sodium:** 103mg | **Carbs:** 7.1g | **Fiber:** 2.9g | **Sugar:** 4g | **Protein:** 27.4g

Beef, Pork and Lamb Recipes

Garlic Rosemary Pork Chops

Prep time: 10 minutes
Cook time: 30 minutes
Serves: 8

Ingredients:

- 8 pork loin chops
- kosher salt
- Freshly ground black pepper
- 2 tablespoon freshly minced rosemary
- 4 cloves garlic, minced
- 1 cup butter, melted
- 2 tablespoon extra-virgin olive oil

Preparation:

1. Preheat the oven to 375° F. Generously season the pork chops with salt and pepper.
2. Combine the butter, rosemary and garlic in a small bowl. Put aside.
3. In an ovenproof pan, heat the olive oil over medium heat, then add the pork chops. Cook for four minutes until golden brown, flip and cook for another four minutes. Liberally brush pork chops with garlic butter.
4. Place the pan in the oven and cook until cooked through (145° F for medium), ten to 12 minutes. Serve with more garlic butter.

Serving Suggestion: Serve the Garlic Rosemary Pork Chops with salad.

Variation Tip: Use thyme if rosemary is not available.

Nutritional Information per Serving:
Calories: 460| **Fat:** 33g | **Sodium:** 310mg | **Carbs:** 1g | **Fiber:** 0g | **Sugar:** 0g | **Protein:** 39g

Spicy Pork

Prep time: 25 minutes
Cook time: 10 minutes
Serves: 2

Ingredients:

- 2 tablespoons hot chili pastes
- 2 tablespoons soy sauce
- 2 tablespoons brown sugar
- 1 1-inch piece of ginger, peeled and finely grated
- 1 garlic clove, finely grated
- Other stuff:
- 1 1/2 pounds pork tenderloin, very thinly sliced (see notes)
- vegetable oil

Preparation:

1. Stir all the ingredients for the sauce in a glass. Pour the sauce over the pork and let stand 20 minutes to 1 hour.
2. Heat a good pan (cast iron type) over high heat. Just add a little vegetable oil.
3. When the oil is hot and shiny, add the pork in a single layer (you may need to do this in batches). Cook undisturbed for one to two minutes until you get that lovely caramelized appearance. Turn over and repeat to finish.

Serving Suggestion: Serve the Spicy Pork with rice.

Variation Tip: Use lamb as a substitute of pork.

Nutritional Information per Serving:
Calories: 274 | **Fat:** 10.2g | **Sodium:** 673mg | **Carbs:** 6.6g | **Fiber:** 2.9g | **Sugar:** 4g | **Protein:** 37.4g

Korean Ground Beef

Prep time: 05 minutes
Cook time: 10 minutes
Serves: 2

Ingredients:

- ½ pound lean ground beef, macros with 96/4
- 1½ ounces sliced roasted red peppers, from a jar
- 1 tablespoon gochujang
- ½ tablespoon sesame oil
- 1 tablespoon lite soy sauce
- 1 tablespoon swerve brown sugar
- ½ teaspoon crushed red pepper

Preparation:

1. Heat a large skillet with nonstock cooking spray over medium-high heat.
2. Put the minced meat in the pan and separate with a spatula. After the minced meat has cooked for three to four minutes, add the roasted red peppers.
3. Combine remaining ingredients in a bowl until smooth.
4. Add the sauce mixture to the meat when there is hardly any rose left in the meat.
5. Reduce heat to low and simmer for about five minutes, stirring frequently.
6. Serve the meat over rice or with a mixture of vegetables and optionally sprinkle sesame seeds.

Serving Suggestion: Serve the Korean Ground Beef with rice or a mixture of vegetables.

Variation Tip: Use coconut anions as a substitute of soy sauce.

Nutritional Information per Serving:
Calories: 201 | **Fat:** 9g | **Sodium:** 103mg | **Carbs:** 11g | **Fiber:** 2.9g | **Sugar:** 4g | **Protein:** 25g

Sweet Ground Beef and Broccoli

Prep time: 05 minutes
Cook time: 15 minutes
Serves: 12

Ingredients:

- 2 pounds lean ground beef, macros with 93/7
- 12 tablespoons sweet barbecue sauce
- 6 tablespoons Worcestershire Sauce
- 2 teaspoons black pepper
- 12 slices precooked bacon, or raw bacon, cooked
- 2 pounds frozen, Steamtable Broccoli Florets

Preparation:

1. Heat the broccoli in the microwave as directed on the package. If you are using fresh broccoli, steam it or cook it first.
2. Put the minced meat in a large saucepan over medium heat.
3. While the meat is cooking, combine the barbecue and Worcestershire Sauce in a small bowl. Add sauce mixture to ground beef while cooking.
4. Use a knife to cut the bacon into 1-inch pieces before adding it to the pan along with the ground beef and sauce mixture.
5. Cook the meat until it is no longer pink before lowering the heat and adding the broccoli.
6. Stir to incorporate the broccoli before serving.
7. Serve with rice or cauliflower rice, noodles, potatoes, baked beans or straight.

Serving Suggestion: Serve the Sweet Ground Beef and Broccoli with rice or cauliflower rice.

Variation Tip: Add cauliflower and broccoli both.

Nutritional Information per Serving:
Calories: 190 | **Fat:** 8g | **Sodium:** 303mg | **Carbs:** 10g | **Fiber:** 1.9g | **Sugar:** 2g | **Protein:** 20g

Beef Cannelloni

Prep time: 20 minutes
Cook time: 40 minutes
Serves: 2

Ingredients:

For the Cannelloni Filling

- 1 pound ground beef, I used 96/4
- 1 onion, diced
- 4 cloves garlic, minced
- 1/2 teaspoon kosher salt and black pepper, to taste
- 1 cup (248g) low fat ricotta
- 1 tablespoon chopped parsley

For the Shells and Sauce

- 12 sheets oven ready Lasagna,
- 24 ounces jar Marinara
- 1 cup (240 grams) Light Alfredo Sauce, I used Classico
- 1/2 cup (56 grams) shredded parmesan

Preparation:

1. Preheat the oven to 350° F.

Cook the cannelloni filling:

2. Heat a large skillet over medium-high heat with non-stick cooking spray. Add the onion, garlic, meat, salt and pepper. Cook until the meat is no longer pink and cooked through.
3. Remove from the heat and let it cool briefly before adding the ricotta and parsley.

Fill the cannelloni:

4. Once the lasagna sheets are soft (about 15-20 minutes in water), place them on a flat surface and cut them in half.
5. Drain the water from the baking dish and pour about half of the marinara to the bottom of the pan.
6. Fill each half of the lasagna sheet with the meat mixture and roll up tightly. Place them sealed side down on the plate above the marinara.
7. Add the rest of the marinara around the edges and in the spaces between. Follow by Alfredo sauce and parmesan on top. Bake for 25-35 minutes.

Serving Suggestion: Serve the Beef Cannelloni with rice.

Variation Tip: Add pork if you don't like beef.

Nutritional Information per Serving:
Calories: 280 | **Fat:** 8g | **Sodium:** 103mg | **Carbs:** 30g | **Fiber:** 1.9g | **Sugar:** 2g | **Protein:** 24g

Swiss chard & Artichoke Stuffed Pork Chops

Prep time: 10 minutes
Cook time: 25 minutes
Serves: 2

Ingredients:

- 4 ounces cream cheese, softened to room temperature
- 1/6 cup sour cream
- 1/6 cup mayonnaise
- ½ can artichoke hearts, drained and chopped
- 10½ - ounce package frozen Swiss chard
- 1 cloves garlic, minced
- 1 cup shredded mozzarella
- 1/8 cup freshly grated parmesan
- Kosher salt
- Pinch of crushed red pepper flakes
- 2 bone-in pork chops (about 1" thick)
- 1 tablespoon extra-virgin olive oil, divided

Preparation:

1. In a large bowl, combine cream cheese, sour cream, mayonnaise, artichoke hearts, Swiss chard, garlic, mozzarella and parmesan. Season with salt and red pepper flakes.
2. Using a kitchen knife, cut out the pockets in the thickest part of the pork chops and fill them with the cream cheese mixture.
3. In a large skillet, heat one tablespoon of oil over medium heat. Add the pork chops and cook, four minutes per side, until golden brown and cooked through. Repeat with the last two pork chops and serve.

Serving Suggestion: Serve the Stuffed Pork Chops with rice.

Variation Tip: Add spinach as a substitute of Swiss chard.

Nutritional Information per Serving:
Calories: 250 | **Fat:** 11.2g | **Sodium:** 503mg | **Carbs:** 7.1g | **Fiber:** 2.9g | **Sugar:** 6g | **Protein:** 47.4g

Pork Chops with Warm Lemon Vinaigrette

Prep time: 05 minutes
Cook time: 30 minutes
Serves: 2

Ingredients:

- 4 bone-in pork chops, 1" thick
- Kosher salt
- Freshly ground black pepper
- Olive oil
- 1 garlic clove, minced
- 4 sprigs fresh thyme
- 1 lemon, cut into ¼" wheels
- 2 tablespoons unsalted butter, cut in half
- 2 cups baby arugula
- Flaky sea salt

Preparation:

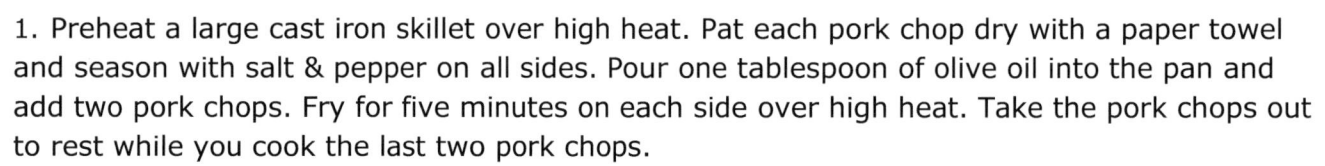

1. Preheat a large cast iron skillet over high heat. Pat each pork chop dry with a paper towel and season with salt & pepper on all sides. Pour one tablespoon of olive oil into the pan and add two pork chops. Fry for five minutes on each side over high heat. Take the pork chops out to rest while you cook the last two pork chops.
2. In the same skillet, reduce the heat to medium. Add one tablespoon of olive oil, garlic, thyme, lemon wedges and half teaspoon of salt. Fry for three to four minutes, until the garlic is tender and the lemons begin to brown. Add the butter and let it melt slowly in a sauce.
3. Garnish the pork chops with fresh arugula and drizzle the pork chops and vegetables with the sauce. Garnish with a pinch of sea salt.

Serving Suggestion: Serve the Pork Chops with cauliflower rice or salad.

Variation Tip: Add garlic powder if garlic is not available.

Nutritional Information per Serving:
Calories: 252 | **Fat:** 13.2g | **Sodium:** 103mg | **Carbs:** 7.1g | **Fiber:** 2.9g | **Sugar:** 4g | **Protein:** 27.4g

Sriracha BBQ Ground Beef and Green Beans

Prep time: 05 minutes
Cook time: 20 minutes
Serves: 2

Ingredients:

- ½ pound ground beef (96/4)
- 2 slices bacon, cut into thin strips
- ¼ tablespoon paprika
- ¼ tablespoon dry mustard
- ¼ teaspoon black pepper
- ¼ teaspoon cumin
- ¼ cup BBQ sauce
- 1 tablespoon Sriracha
- 1 tablespoon Worcestershire Sauce
- 1 cup beef broth
- 4 ounces green beans

Preparation:

1. Place the minced meat and bacon in a large saucepan over medium heat. Combine the dry mustard, paprika, black pepper and cumin and add to the pan. Cook until meat is no longer pink and bacon is cooked through, about eight to ten minutes.
2. Mix the BBQ sauce, Sriracha, Worcestershire sauce and beef broth together. As soon as the meat is cooked, add the liquid ingredients and mix everything together.
3. Add the green beans to the pan and dip them in the liquid. Cook over medium to high heat, stirring occasionally, for eight to ten minutes or until the liquid ingredients have thickened to the consistency of a sauce.
4. Serve over toasted sesame rice, chives or your choice of toppings.

Serving Suggestion: Serve the BBQ Ground Beef and Green Beans with rice.

Variation Tip: Use Broccoli if green beans are not available.

Nutritional Information per Serving:
Calories: 250| **Fat:** 7g | **Sodium:** 203mg | **Carbs:** 17.1g | **Fiber:** 2.9g | **Sugar:** 4g | **Protein:** 27g

Grilled Lamb Chops

Prep time: 10 minutes
Cook time: 30 minutes
Serves: 2

Ingredients:

- 2 lamb racks
- 1 tablespoon olive oil
- 1 tablespoon garlic (minced)
- 1/2 teaspoon salt
- Pinch ground pepper
- Fresh rosemary (about 1 inch each)

Preparation:

1. Cut each rack of lamb into four pieces of two bones, leaving one bone with an equal amount of meat.
2. Combine olive oil, garlic, salt, pepper and rosemary. Completely spread the rack of lamb and marinate in the refrigerator for two hours.
3. Preheat the grill and cook the chops over low heat. Flip the chops to cook on both sides. Use a meat thermometer to check when the grates are ready.

Serving Suggestion: Serve the Grilled Lamb Chops with rice.

Variation Tip: Use thyme as a substitute of rosemary.

Nutritional Information per Serving:
Calories: 190 | **Fat:** 10g | **Sodium:** 350mg | **Carbs:** 1g | **Fiber:** 0g | **Sugar:** 0g | **Protein:** 22g

Roast Lamb

Prep time: 15 minutes
Cook time: 60 minutes
Serves: 5

Ingredients:

- 1.5 pounds lamb leg
- ½ tablespoon olive oil
- 1 sprigs rosemary
- 2 cloves garlic crushed

Preparation:

1. Make small incisions in the meat with a knife.
2. Rub the meat with oil.
3. Put the sprigs of rosemary in the cups.
4. Bake at 180° C (350° F) for one hour 30 minutes for half-cooked meat.
5. Let the meat rest for 15 minutes before slicing it.

Serving Suggestion: Serve the Roast Lamb with salad.

Variation Tip: Add garlic powder if fresh garlic is not available.

Nutritional Information per Serving:
Calories: 413 | **Fat:** 29g | **Sodium:** 342mg | **Carbs:** 0.4g | **Fiber:** 0.1g | **Sugar:** 0.1g | **Protein:** 36g

Vegetarian Mains Recipes

Chickpeas Meatball

Prep time: 15 minutes
Cook time: 25 minutes
Serves: 4

Ingredients:

- 1 cup chickpeas - reserve chickpea liquid if using canned
- 2 tablespoons ground flax seed
- 3 tablespoon water
- ¼ cup breadcrumbs
- ¼ tablespoon garlic powder
- 1 teaspoon onion powder
- ½ teaspoon dried parsley
- ½ teaspoon marjoram
- ¼ teaspoon salt - or to taste
- ¼ teaspoon basil
- 1/8 teaspoon black pepper

Preparation:

1. If you are using dried chickpeas, let them soak for four hours. Cook, about 45 minutes to an hour. Skip to next step if using canned chickpeas!
2. Throw in the chickpeas and peel the skins of anyone you have patience with. Blend the chickpeas in a blender until they fall apart.
3. Mix ground flax seeds with six tablespoons of water. Let stand ten to 15 minutes.
4. Mix the chickpeas and flax seed mixture together.
5. Mix the remaining ingredients. If the mixture is too sticky, add more breadcrumbs, half a tablespoon at a time. If it is too dry, add a little oil or chickpeas. You want a consistency that easily rolls into balls without sticking to your hands or cracking.
6. Shape the chickpea mixture into meatballs and place in a greased baking dish or lined with parchment paper.
7. Bake the chickpea balls in a 450° F oven for 20-25 minutes and turn them halfway through cooking. They will turn golden and crisp on the outside when cooked!

Serving Suggestion: Serve the Chickpeas Meatballs with pasta.

Variation Tip: Add broccoli if you like.

Nutritional Information per Serving:
Calories: 225 | **Fat:** 4.1g | **Sodium:** 63mg | **Carbs:** 36.4g | **Fiber:** 9.7g | **Sugar:** 6.1g | **Protein:** 11.1g

Tomato Quinoa Soup with Roasted Chickpeas

Prep time: 10 minutes
Cook time: 55 minutes
Serves: 2

Ingredients:

- 1 tablespoon olive oil
- ½ cup diced onion
- 2 carrots, diced
- ½ cup dry quinoa, rinsed
- 1 28-ounce cans crushed tomatoes
- 2 cups vegetable broth
- 1 tablespoon tomato paste
- 3 cloves garlic, sliced
- ½ tablespoon dry oregano
- ½ tablespoon dry basil
- 1 teaspoon crushed rosemary
- ¼ teaspoon crushed red pepper
- Salt and pepper
- 1 cup chopped spinach

Preparation:

1. Place olive oil, onion and carrots in a pan preheated over medium heat. Cook for five minutes or until onion is translucent. Add the quinoa and cook for five minutes or until the grains are flavorful.
2. Add the crushed tomatoes, vegetable broth, tomato paste, garlic, oregano, basil, rosemary, crushed red pepper, salt and pepper. Bring to a boil, then reduce the heat to low to medium and simmer for 40 minutes, or until the barley is tender but still slightly al dente. Add the spinach and cook for five minutes or until just tender.
3. Serve with roasted chickpeas and vegan cheese if desired.

Serving Suggestion: Serve the Tomato Quinoa Soup with pasta.

Variation Tip: Use barley if you don't have quinoa.

Nutritional Information per Serving:
Calories: 237 | **Fat:** 5.7g | **Sodium:** 746mg | **Carbs:** 36.7g | **Fiber:** 9.7g | **Sugar:** 14.1g | **Protein:** 11.2g

Tofu Stir-Fry

Prep time: 05 minutes
Cook time: 25 minutes
Serves: 12

Ingredients:

- 14 ounces soba noodles, uncooked (use rice noodles for gluten-free)
- 24 ounces shelled edamame beans
- 2 tablespoon coconut oil
- 2 (14-ounce package) firm tofu, drained
- 4 stalks green onion, sliced
- 2 teaspoon curry powder
- 1 cup coconut milk
- ½ cup almond milk
- ¼ cup agave syrup
- 2 carrots, shredded
- ½ cup chopped cashews

Preparation:

1. Cook the soba noodles in lightly salted water according to package directions. Drain and immediately rinse with cold water until it cools, set aside.
2. Cook the edamame beans over medium heat for five minutes or until cooked through. Drain and set aside.
3. Meanwhile: Cut the tofu into ½ inch cubes. Heat the coconut oil in a nonstock skillet or skillet over medium heat, add the tofu. Cook and turn as needed until lightly browned, seven to ten minutes. Drain off excess liquid and reduce heat to medium.
4. Add the green onions and the curry powder, cook for one minute. Add the rest of the ingredients and simmer for ten minutes or until the sauce is a little thick. Add the cooked soba noodles and edamame beans and cook until heated through. Garnish with more cashews before serving, if desired.

Serving Suggestion: Serve the Tofu Stir-Fry with noodles.

Variation Tip: Use rice noodles if gluten free.

Nutritional Information per Serving:
Calories: 468 | **Fat:** 23.2g | **Sodium:** 305mg | **Carbs:** 50.7g | **Fiber:** 6.6g | **Sugar:** 4.8g | **Protein:** 21.2g

Enchilada Zucchini Boats

Prep time: 15 minutes
Cook time: 60 minutes
Serves: 2

Ingredients:

- ½ tablespoon oil
- ¼ of a sweet onion
- ¼ red bell pepper
- 2 cloves of garlic, minced
- 1/8 teaspoon of cumin
- 1/8 teaspoon of dried oregano
- 1/8 teaspoon of paprika
- 1/8 teaspoon of salt
- ½ ounce can of black beans, drained and rinsed
- 2 medium zucchinis
- ¾ cup of enchilada sauce

Preparation:

1. Preheat the oven to 400° F and lightly grease a baking dish.
2. Prepare your zucchini by cutting it in half and carefully scraping most of the inside of the zucchini and discarding it. You want the zucchini zest to be about ¼-inch-thick after removing the inside.
3. Heat the olive oil in a pan over medium heat, then add the onion and pepper and sauté for for minutes. Add the garlic and spices and sauté for another two minutes.
4. Add the black beans and cook for another three minutes, until the black beans are heated through. Put out the fire.
5. Distribute the mixture into zucchini evenly and place in a greased baking dish.
6. Top the zucchini with the enchilada sauce.
7. Optional: Top with vegan cheese.
8. Bake for 30-35 minutes at 400° F.
9. Let cool a bit and ENJOY!

Serving Suggestion: Serve the Enchilada Zucchini Boat with salad.

Variation Tip: Use squash if not finding zucchini.

Nutritional Information per Serving:
Calories: 114 | **Fat:** 4.4g | **Sodium:** 175mg | **Carbs:** 19.5g | **Fiber:** 6.6g | **Sugar:** 4.9g | **Protein:** 3.6g

Garlic Teriyaki Tempeh and Broccoli

Prep time: 05 minutes
Cook time: 10 minutes
Serves: 6

Ingredients:

- ¼ cup olive or avocado oil used as needed
- 16 ounce package of tempeh cut into ¼ inch strips
- ½ cup nutritional yeast flakes
- 1 pound of fresh broccoli chopped into bite-size florets
- 8 garlic cloves minced
- Cooked rice quinoa or cauliflower rice for serving
- Chopped scallions and sesame seeds for garnish

Teriyaki Sauce:

- 1 tablespoon olive or avocado oil
- ¼ cup low sodium tamari or soy sauce
- ½ tablespoon maple syrup
- 2 cloves of garlic minced
- ½ teaspoon fresh ginger grated or minced

Preparation:

1. Prepare the sauce: Whisk all the ingredients for the teriyaki sauce in a small bowl and set aside.
2. Whisk teriyaki sauce in a small glass bowl.
3. Fry: In a large skillet over medium-low heat, brown the tempeh strips in a little oil and gradually add more oil so that the pan does not dry out.

Tempeh Teriyaki in a skillet:

4. Add the sauce: Once the tempeh is golden, add the teriyaki sauce and nutritional yeast and toss to coat the tempeh.
5. Add the broccoli - toss the broccoli florets and garlic in the pan. Sear the mixture for about ten minutes, turning it occasionally.
6. Serve: Remove from heat as soon as the broccoli is tender, crisp and light in color. Serve immediately over quinoa, rice or cauliflower rice with chives and sesame seeds for garnish.

Serving Suggestion: Serve the Teriyaki Tempeh and Broccoli with salad.

Variation Tip: Use tofu if tempeh is not available.

Nutritional Information per Serving:
Calories: 313 | **Fat:** 20g | **Sodium:** 981mg | **Carbs:** 21g | **Fiber:** 5g | **Sugar:** 3g | **Protein:** 21g

Red Lentil Stew with Chickpeas

Prep time: 10 minutes.
Cook time: 30 minutes
Serves: 12

Ingredients:

- 1 tablespoon olive oil or ¼ cup water/veg broth
- 1 large yellow onion, diced
- 5 cloves garlic, minced
- 1 ½ inch knob fresh ginger, minced
- 1 – 2 tablespoon curry (yellow), to taste
- 1 teaspoon cumin
- 1 teaspoon turmeric
- Himalayan salt to taste
- 1 – 2 teaspoon red pepper flakes, optional
- 1 cup fresh tomatoes, diced
- 2 cups dry red lentils, rinsed and picked over
- 1 ½ cups cooked chickpeas
- 6 cups water or vegetable broth, + more as needed
- 4 cups spinach, julienned
- Juice of one lemon, optional

Preparation:

1. In a large saucepan, heat oil over medium heat, sauté onion, garlic and ginger until onions becomes translucent, about five minutes. Add the spices, tomatoes, lentils, chickpeas and six cups of liquid, bring to a boil, cover, reduce heat and simmer for about 30 minutes.
2. Add the spinach and possibly the lemon juice, continue cooking for ten minutes or until the cabbage is tender and wilted.

Serving Suggestion: Serve the Red Lentil Stew with rice.

Variation Tip: Use kale if spinach is not available.

Nutritional Information per Serving:
Calories: 530 | **Fat:** 6.9g | **Sodium:** 42mg | **Carbs:** 7.4g | **Fiber:** 3.1g | **Sugar:** 0.1g | **Protein:** 30.5g

Grilled Cauliflower Steak

Prep time: 10 minutes
Cook time: 20 minutes
Serves: 2

Ingredients:

- 1 large head of cauliflower, sliced lengthwise through the core into 4 'steaks'
- 2 tablespoon fresh lemon juice
- 1 tablespoon olive oil
- Sea salt

For the Romesco Sauce:

- ¼ cup slivered almonds
- 1/2 a large tomato on the vine, chopped
- 1/2 cup thinly sliced roasted red peppers, packed
- 1/2 tablespoon fresh lemon juice
- 1 teaspoon garlic, minced
- ¼ teaspoon sea salt
- ¼ teaspoon ground cumin
- Sliced parsley, for garnish

Preparation:

1. Preheat your oven to 350° F. Spread the almonds on a small baking sheet and bake for about three to five minutes, until golden brown. Watch them carefully as they burn quickly. Put aside. Preheat your grill to medium heat.
2. Place the cauliflower fillets on a cutting board and combine the lemon juice and oil in a small bowl. Brush the cauliflower with half the oil mixture and sprinkle salt.
3. Place the cauliflower "fillets" oil side down on the grill and cook, about eight to nine minutes, until charred and tender. Then rub the rest of the oil mixture on the "fillets" and turn them over. Cook soft and tender with a fork, another eight to ten minutes.
4. While the cauliflower is cooking, place 1/2 of the tomato in a small food processor and process until cracked and smooth.
5. Add all the other sauce ingredients, including the toasted almonds, and mix until smooth and creamy.
6. Serve the sauce over the cauliflower and garnish with parsley.

Serving Suggestion: Serve Grilled Cauliflower Steak with salad and quinoa.

Variation Tip: Use broccoli also.

Nutritional Information per Serving:
Calories: 111 | **Fat:** 7g | **Sodium:** 251mg | **Carbs:** 10.4g | **Fiber:** 4.7g | **Sugar:** 3.8g | **Protein:** 3.6g

Cauliflower Fried Rice

Prep time: 15 minutes
Cook time: 60 minutes
Serves: 5

Ingredients:

- 1 16-ounce block firm tofu
- 2 tablespoons coconut aminos
- 1 tablespoon vegetable oil
- 1 tablespoon sesame oil
- 1 clove garlic minced
- 5 cups chopped broccoli or veggie of choice
- ¼ cup mayonnaise
- ¼ cup plain Greek yogurt
- 2 to 4 Tbsp sriracha

Preparation:

1. Tofu: Squeeze the tofu to remove excess moisture. Cut into bite-sized cubes and add to a large skillet along with vegetable oil, sesame oil and garlic. Fry until golden and crisp on all sides over medium/high heat.
2. Vegetables: Place the broccoli in a microwave-safe plate and drizzle with a little water. Cover with plastic wrap and microwave on high power for two to three minutes, or until light green and tender.
3. Sauce: Stir to combine mayonnaise, yogurt and sriracha.
4. Assembly: Pour the sauce evenly at the bottom of five mason jars, then add the rice, vegetables and tofu. Store in the refrigerator for up to five days. When ready to eat, heat it in the microwave for two to three minutes.

Serving Suggestion: Serve the cauliflower rice with salad.

Variation Tip: Use tempeh if you don't like tofu.

Nutritional Information per Serving:
Calories: 331 | **Fat:** 22.2g | **Sodium:** 963mg | **Carbs:** 21.4g | **Fiber:** 5.9g | **Sugar:** 7.3g | **Protein:** 15.7g

Sweet Potato Chili

Prep time: 15 minutes
Cook time: 60 minutes
Serves: 2

Ingredients:

- 1 teaspoon olive oil
- ½ red onion (sliced)
- 1 garlic cloves (minced)
- 2 cups sweet potato (peeled & diced)
- ½ teaspoon chili powder/flakes
- 1 teaspoon cumin
- ½ tin kidney beans (drained)
- 1 teaspoon soy sauce
- 2 cups water
- 1 tablespoon tomato puree
- Salt & pepper to taste

Preparation:

1. In a large skillet, heat the olive oil over medium heat. Add the red onion and garlic and sauté for a few minutes.
2. Add the sweet potato cubes and season with salt and pepper. Mix well, then pour in the water, cover the pot with a lid and simmer for 30 minutes.
3. Now add the chili powder and cumin, stir in the spices and cover again for five minutes.
4. Remove the lid and mash the sweet potato with a potato masher until smooth and free of lumps. Add the beans, soy sauce and tomato puree and mix until well-blended. Replace the lid and simmer another five minutes to warm the beans.

Serving Suggestion: Serve the chili with salad.

Variation Tip: Add potatoes if sweet potatoes are not available.

Nutritional Information per Serving:
Calories: 221 | **Fat:** 2.9g | **Sodium:** 342mg | **Carbs:** 39.4g | **Fiber:** 0.1g | **Sugar:** 0.1g | **Protein:** 7.6g

Avocado Pesto Zucchini Noodles

Prep time: 10 minutes
Cook time: 10 minutes
Serves: 2

Ingredients:

- 2 ounces whole wheat spaghetti noodles
- 1 medium sized zucchini, spiralized
- 1 cup sliced cherry tomatoes
- ½ cup Avocado Pesto
- Salt and pepper, to taste

Preparation:

1. Bring a large pot of water to a boil and cook the pasta according to the directions on the package. Drain the pasta and rinse with cold water.
2. Return the noodles to the pan with the zucchini noodles and cherry tomatoes. Add the avocado pesto and stir until combined. Add salt and pepper to taste and enjoy immediately.

Serving Suggestion: Serve the Avocado Pesto Zucchini Noodles with salad.

Variation Tip: Use any kind of noodles.

Nutritional Information per Serving:
Calories: 178 | **Fat:** 4.5g | **Sodium:** 195mg | **Carbs:** 28g | **Fiber:** 4.7g | **Sugar:** 4.6g | **Protein:** 9.6g

Salads, Snacks and Sides Recipes

Strawberry Caprese Pasta Salad

Prep time: 05 minutes
Cook time: 10 minutes
Serves: 2

Ingredients:

- 4 ounces whole wheat penne
- 1/8 cup apple cider vinegar
- 1/8 cup mint, finely chopped, plus small leaves for serving
- 1 tablespoon olive oil
- ¼ small onion, finely chopped
- 6 ounces small strawberries
- 2 ounces white cheddar, halved if large
- Kosher salt and pepper

Preparation:

1. Cook pasta according to package directions. Drain and run under cold water to cool to room temperature.
2. In a large bowl, combine the vinegar, mint, oil, onion and a pinch of salt and pepper.
3. Add the noodles to the bowl and toss to coat. Add strawberries and cheddar. Season with salt and pepper and garnish with additional mint if desired.

Serving Suggestion: Serve the Strawberry Caprese Pasta Salad with quinoa.

Variation Tip: Use any kind of pasta.

Nutritional Information per Serving:
Calories: 402 | **Fat:** 14.5g | **Sodium:** 195mg | **Carbs:** 53g | **Fiber:** 7g | **Sugar:** 0g | **Protein:** 13g

Lentil and Steak Salad

Prep time: 10 minutes
Cook time: 10 minutes
Serves: 2

Ingredients:

- 1½ tablespoon olive oil
- 6 ounces sirloin steak (about 1-inch thick) trimmed of excess fat
- ½ tablespoon fresh lemon juice
- ½ teaspoon Dijon mustard
- ¼ teaspoon maple syrup
- 1/8 medium red onion, finely chopped
- ½-ounce can lentils, rinsed
- 1/8 small red cabbage (about 8 oz), cored and chopped
- ¼ cup flat-leaf parsley, roughly chopped
- 1 red grapefruits
- 3 cups baby spinach
- Kosher salt and pepper

Preparation:

1. Heat ½ tablespoon oil in a large cast iron skillet over medium heat. Season the steak with 1/8 teaspoon of salt and pepper and cook, four to six minutes per side, until cooked through. Place on a cutting board and let sit for at least five minutes before cutting into one inch size.
2. Meanwhile, combine lemon juice, Dijon mustard, maple syrup, remaining one tablespoon oil and 1/8 teaspoon salt and pepper each in a large bowl. Add the onion, lentils, red cabbage and parsley and mix.
3. Remove the skin and white pulp from the grapefruit, cut in half and thin slices. Toss grapefruit, spinach and steak in a salad.

Serving Suggestion: Serve the Lentil and Steak Salad with noodles.

Variation Tip: Use arugula as a substitute of spinach.

Nutritional Information per Serving:
Calories: 330 | **Fat:** 12g | **Sodium:** 195mg | **Carbs:** 32g | **Fiber:** 10g | **Sugar:** 4.6g | **Protein:** 25g

Green Bowl with Chicken

Prep time: 10 minutes
Cook time: 10 minutes
Serves: 2

Ingredients:

- 2 teaspoon olive oil
- 2 small shallots, minced
- 1 teaspoon sea salt
- 2 cups broccoli slaw
- 2 cups chopped asparagus
- 4 cups baby spinach
- Finely grated zest of 1 orange
- 1 teaspoon zaatar
- 6 ounces leftover cooked chicken, shredded
- ½ avocado, pitted, peeled and sliced
- ½ cup green goddess dressing (any kind)
- Finely grated zest of 1 lemon
- 1/8 cup minced fresh herbs

Preparation:

1. Heat olive oil in a large skillet over medium heat.
2. Add the shallot and sea salt and cook, stirring frequently, until the shallot begins to turn translucent.
3. Add the broccoli slaw and asparagus and cook, stirring occasionally, until the asparagus is tender and light green.
4. Add the spinach, orange zest and zaatar and cook until the spinach is tender. Add the chicken and cook until heated through.
5. Transfer to a bowl and serve with avocado, dressing, lemon zest and fresh herbs.

Serving Suggestion: Serve the Green Bowl with Chicken with chips.

Variation Tip: You can use turkey as a substitute of chicken.

Nutritional Information per Serving:
Calories: 443 | **Fat:** 19g | **Sodium:** 195mg | **Carbs:** 22g | **Fiber:** 4.7g | **Sugar:** 4.6g | **Protein:** 32g

Turkey Avocado Cobb Salad

Prep time: 05 minutes
Cook time: 10 minutes
Serves: 2

Ingredients:

- ½ pound turkey breast cutlets
- 1 tablespoon olive oil
- 1/8 tablespoon salt
- 1 tablespoon cider vinegar
- ½ teaspoon Dijon mustard
- 4 cup baby spinach leaves
- 2 slices cooked reduced sodium turkey bacon, crumbled
- ¼ ripe avocado, cut into 1/2" cubes
- 2 cherry tomatoes, halved
- ½ ounce feta cheese, crumbled

Preparation:

1. Preheat the grill pan over medium heat for two minutes. Brush the turkey with one teaspoon of oil and sprinkle with half the salt. cook the turkey for four minutes, turn and continue cooking until the center is cooked and the juices are clear, another three minutes. To cut into pieces.
2. For the dressing, combine the vinegar, Dijon mustard, one tablespoon of water and the remaining two teaspoons of oil and 1/8 of a teaspoon of salt in a glass jar. Shake well.
3. In a large bowl, toss the spinach with two tablespoons of the dressing. Place the turkey, bacon, avocado, tomatoes and cheese on top of the spinach. Pour the remaining dressing over the salad and season with black pepper.

Serving Suggestion: Serve the Turkey Avocado Cobb Salad with noodles.

Variation Tip: Use blue chesses as a substitute of feta.

Nutritional Information per Serving:
Calories: 288 | **Fat:** 13g | **Sodium:** 472mg | **Carbs:** 10g | **Fiber:** 4.7g | **Sugar:** 1g | **Protein:** 34g

Beet and Pumpkin Salad

Prep time: 10 minutes
Cook time: 10 minutes
Serves: 2

Ingredients:

- 1 pumpkin
- grapeseed oil
- 2 beets (with green tops)
- 1 teaspoon cumin
- ½ cup cooked quinoa
- 1 bunch arugula, chopped

Dressing

- 1 cup chopped carrots
- ¼ cup peeled and chopped ginger
- 1 garlic clove, sliced
- 2 shallots, sliced
- 1 tablespoon tamari (or low sodium soy sauce)
- 1 tablespoon sesame oil
- 1 tablespoon maple syrup
- 1 teaspoon Dijon mustard
- 2 tablespoon rice vinegar
- ¼ cups grapeseed oil
- 2–3 tablespoon water

Preparation:

1. Heat the oven to 350° F.
2. Cut the pumpkin in half. Scrape off seed and pulp with a spoon. Spread the pumpkin seeds on a baking sheet lined with parchment paper and remove the excess pulp. Drizzle with oil and cumin and season with salt and pepper. Discard to combine. Bake until the seeds start to brown, 20 to 25 minutes.
3. Meanwhile, cut the pumpkin into small pieces and place it on a baking sheet lined with parchment paper. Brush the slices with a little oil and season with salt and pepper.
4. Remove and store the beetroot greens. Peel the beetroot and cut it into square pieces or thin slices. Place the chopped beets on a baking sheet lined with parchment paper, brush with oil and season with salt and pepper.
5. When the seeds are cooked, take them out of the oven and let them cool. Increase oven temperature to 400° F. Place the pumpkin and beetroot in the oven and bake for 40 to 45 minutes, until tender.
6. Meanwhile, prepare the vinaigrette: Place the carrots in a food processor and blend until crumbly. Add the ginger, garlic, shallots, tamari (or soy sauce), sesame oil, mustard, maple

syrup and vinegar. Pulse until combined, then slowly add oil until dressing is completely emulsified. Add water to dressing until desired consistency is achieved.

7. When the pumpkin and beets are cooked, take them out of the oven and let them cool before assembling the salad.

8. Pour the vinaigrette over the quinoa and stir. Chop the beet leaves (without the stems) and add them to the quinoa with the arugula. Garnish with beets, pumpkin seeds and a few slices of pumpkin. Drizzle with more dressing and serve.

Serving Suggestion: Serve the Beet and Pumpkin Salad with noodles.

Variation Tip: Use kale if arugula is not available.

Nutritional Information per Serving:
Calories: 340 | **Fat:** 23g | **Sodium:** 260mg | **Carbs:** 31g | **Fiber:** 5g | **Sugar:** 4.6g | **Protein:** 8g

Avocado Chips

Prep time: 10 minutes
Cook time: 30 minutes
Serves: 8

Ingredients:

- 1 large ripe avocado
- 3/4 cups freshly grated feta
- 1 teaspoon lemon juice
- 1/2 teaspoon garlic powder
- 1/2 teaspoon Italian seasoning
- Kosher salt
- Freshly ground black pepper

Preparation:

1. Preheat the oven to 325° F and line two baking sheets with parchment paper. In a medium bowl, mash the avocado with a fork until smooth. Add the feta, lemon juice, garlic powder and Italian seasonings. Season with salt and pepper.
2. Place a tablespoon-sized teaspoon of the mixture on a baking sheet, leaving about three inches between each spoon. Flatten each scoop to 3" wide with the back of a spoon or measuring cup. Bake for about 30 minutes until crisp and golden, then cool completely. Serve at room temperature.

Serving Suggestion: Serve the Avocado Chips with mayo.

Variation Tip: Use parmesan cheese if you don't like feta.

Nutritional Information per Serving:
Calories: 120 | **Fat:** 10g | **Sodium:** 230mg | **Carbs:** 4g | **Fiber:** 2g | **Sugar:** 0g | **Protein:** 7g

Jalapeño Pepper Egg Cups

Prep time: 15 minutes
Cook time: 45 minutes
Serves: 6

Ingredients:

- 6 slices bacon
- 5 large eggs
- 1/8 cup sour cream
- ¼ cup shredded Cheddar
- ¼ cup shredded mozzarella
- 1 jalapeño, 1 minced and 1 thinly sliced
- ½ teaspoon garlic powder
- Kosher salt
- Freshly ground black pepper
- Non-stick cooking spray

Preparation:

1. Preheat the oven to 375° F. Bake the bacon in a large skillet over medium heat until lightly browned but still pliable. Set aside on a paper towel-lined plate to drain.
2. In a large bowl, combine the eggs, sour cream, cheese, chopped jalapeños and garlic powder. Season with salt and pepper.
3. Grease a muffin tin with non-stick cooking spray. Cover each well with a slice of bacon, then pour the egg mixture about two-thirds of the way up into each muffin pan. Top each muffin with a slice of jalapeño.
4. Bake for 20 minutes or until eggs are no longer moist. Let it cool a bit before removing it from the muffin pan.

Serving Suggestion: Serve the Jalapeño Popper Egg Cups with ketchup.

Variation Tip: Use sweet bell pepper as a substitute of jalapeño.

Nutritional Information per Serving:
Calories: 186 | **Fat:** 13.5g | **Sodium:** 547mg | **Carbs:** 1.2g | **Fiber:** 0.1g | **Sugar:** 0.5g | **Protein:** 14g

Burger Fat Bombs

Prep time: 15 minutes
Cook time: 30 minutes
Serves: 10

Ingredients:

- Cooking spray
- ½ pound ground beef
- ¼ teaspoon garlic powder
- Kosher salt
- Freshly ground black pepper
- 1 tablespoon cold butter, cut into 20 pieces
- 1 ounce cheddar, cut into 20 pieces
- Lettuce leaves, for serving
- Thinly sliced tomatoes, for serving
- Mustard, for serving

Preparation:

1. Preheat the oven to 375° F and grease a mini muffin tin with cooking spray. In a medium bowl, season the meat with the garlic powder, salt and pepper.
2. Evenly press one teaspoon of beef into bottom of each muffin pan, completely covering bottom. Put a piece of butter on top, then squeeze one teaspoon of beef over the butter to coat it completely.
3. In each cup, place a piece of cheddar cheese over the meat, then press the rest of the meat onto the cheese to cover it completely.
4. Bake until meat is cooked through, about 15 minutes. Let it cool slightly.
5. Carefully use a metal spatula to remove each patty from the box. Serve with lettuce leaves, tomatoes and mustard.

Serving Suggestion: Serve the Burger Fat Bombs with ketchup.

Variation Tip: You can use pork meat also.

Nutritional Information per Serving:
Calories: 80 | Fat: 7g | Sodium: 45mg | Carbs: 0g | Fiber: 0g | Sugar: 0g | Protein: 5g

Cucumber Sushi

Prep time: 15 minutes
Cook time: 20 minutes
Serves: 2

Ingredients:

For the Sushi

- 1 medium cucumbers, halved
- 1/8 avocado, thinly sliced
- ¼ red bell pepper, thinly sliced
- ¼ yellow bell pepper, thinly sliced
- 1 small carrot, thinly sliced

For the Dipping Sauce

- ¼ cup mayonnaise
- ½ tablespoon sriracha
- ½ teaspoon soy sauce

Preparation:

1. Using a teaspoon, scoop out the seeds from the center of the cucumbers until they are completely hollow.
2. Squeeze the avocado into the center of the cucumber and press it into the cucumber with a butter knife. Then slide in the peppers and carrots until the cucumber is completely filled with vegetables.
3. Prepare a dip: Combine the mayonnaise, sriracha and soy sauce in a small bowl. Whisk to combine.
4. Cut the cucumber slices into one thick piece and serve with the sauce on the side.

Serving Suggestion: Serve Cucumber Sushi with wasabi.

Variation Tip: Use green bell pepper as well.

Nutritional Information per Serving:
Calories: 190 | **Fat:** 4.5g | **Sodium:** 240mg | **Carbs:** 9g | **Fiber:** 3g | **Sugar:** 5g | **Protein:** 1g

Bacon Asparagus Bites

Prep time: 10 minutes
Cook time: 30 minutes
Serves: 12

Ingredients:

- 12 slices bacon, cut into thirds
- 10 ounces cream cheese, softened to room temperature
- 2 garlic cloves, minced
- Freshly ground black pepper
- Kosher salt
- 18 asparagus spears, blanched

Preparation:

1. Preheat the oven to 400° F and line one middle plate with parchment paper.
2. Cook the Bacon: In a large skillet over medium heat, cook the bacon until most of the fat is cooked but not crisp. Remove from the pan and drain on a plate lined with paper towels.
3. Combine the cream cheese with the garlic in a small bowl and season with salt & pepper. Stir until just combined.
4. Assemble Bites: Spread about 1/2 tablespoon of cream cheese on each slice of bacon. Place the asparagus in the center and roll the bacon until the ends of the bacon meet. When all the bites are ready, place them on a prepared baking sheet and bake for five minutes until the bacon is crisp and the cream cheese is piping hot.

Serving Suggestion: Serve the Bacon Asparagus Bites with salad.

Variation Tip: Use ham if bacon is not available.

Nutritional Information per Serving:
Calories: 130 | **Fat:** 4.5g | **Sodium:** 210mg | **Carbs:** 3g | **Fiber:** 1g | **Sugar:** 1g | **Protein:** 5g

Drinks and Beverages Recipes

Berry Avocado Breakfast Smoothie

Prep time: 10 minutes
Cook time: 00 minutes
Serves: 2

Ingredients:

- 1 cup of water
- 1/2 cup of frozen mixed berries (strawberries, blueberries, and raspberries)
- Half of an avocado
- 2 cups of spinach
- 2 tablespoon chia seeds

Preparation:

1. Put all ingredients into blender and blend until smooth.

Serving Suggestion: Serve the Berry Avocado Breakfast Smoothie with sandwich.

Variation Tip: Use kale if spinach is not available.

Nutritional Information per Serving:
Calories: 143 | **Fat:** 11g | **Sodium:** 30mg | **Carbs:** 9.1g | **Fiber:** 1g | **Sugar:** 4.7g | **Protein:** 4.3g

Chocolate Peanut Butter Smoothie

Prep time: 10 minutes
Cook time: 30 minutes
Serves: 1

Ingredients:

- 1 cup unsweetened coconut milk
- 2 tablespoon creamy peanut butter
- 1 tablespoon unsweetened cocoa powder
- ¼ cup of heavy cream

Preparation:

1. Put all ingredients into blender and blend until smooth.

Serving Suggestion: Serve the Chocolate Peanut Butter Smoothie with chips.

Variation Tip: Use almond milk if you don't like coconut milk.

Nutritional Information per Serving:
Calories: 345 | **Fat:** 31g | **Sodium:** 210mg | **Carbs:** 13g | **Fiber:** 4g | **Sugar:** 1g | **Protein:** 11g

Strawberry Zucchini Hemp Smoothie

Prep time: 10 minutes
Cook time: 00 minutes
Serves: 1

Ingredients:

- 1 cup water
- 1/2 cup frozen strawberries
- 1 cup chopped zucchini, frozen or raw
- 3 tablespoon hemp seeds

Preparation:

1. Put all ingredients into blender and blend until smooth.

Serving Suggestion: Serve the Strawberry Zucchini Hemp Smoothie with chips.

Variation Tip: Use chia seeds.

Nutritional Information per Serving:
Calories: 169 | **Fat:** 10.5g | **Sodium:** 18mg | **Carbs:** 11.8g | **Fiber:** 3.5g | **Sugar:** 6.4g | **Protein:** 9g

Coconut Blackberry Mint Smoothie

Prep time: 10 minutes
Cook time: 30 minutes
Serves: 12

Ingredients:

- 1/2 cup (120 ml) of unsweetened full-fat coconut milk
- 1/2 cup (70 grams) of frozen blackberries
- 2 tablespoon of shredded coconut
- 5–10 mint leaves

Preparation:

1. Put all ingredients into blender and blend until smooth.

Serving Suggestion: Serve the coconut blackberry mint smoothie with chips.

Variation Tip: Add chia seeds if you like.

Nutritional Information per Serving:
Calories: 364 | **Fat:** 32.7g | **Sodium:** 36mg | **Carbs:** 19.3g | **Fiber:** 10.8g | **Sugar:** 8.1g | **Protein:** 5.7g

Cucumber Green Smoothie

Prep time: 10 minutes
Cook time: 00 minutes
Serves: 1

Ingredients:

- 1/2 cup water
- 1/2 cup ice
- 1 cup sliced cucumber
- 1 cup kale
- 1 tablespoon lemon juice
- 2 tablespoon milled flax seeds

Preparation:

1. Put all ingredients into blender and blend until smooth.

Serving Suggestion: Serve the cucumber Green Smoothie with chips

Variation Tip: You can use spinach as a substitute of cucumber.

Nutritional Information per Serving:
Calories: 112 | **Fat:** 5.2g | **Sodium:** 38mg | **Carbs:** 15.1g | **Fiber:** 5.6g | **Sugar:** 2.1g | **Protein:** 5.8g

Nutmeg Strawberries Smoothie

Prep time: 10 minutes
Cook time: 00 minutes
Serves: 1

Ingredients:

- 1 cup unsweetened soy milk
- 1/2 cup frozen strawberries
- 1 cup spinach
- 2 tablespoons peanut butter
- 1/8 teaspoon nutmeg, or more to taste

Preparation:

1. Put all ingredients into blender and blend until smooth.

Serving Suggestion: Serve the Nutmeg Strawberries Smoothie with roasted chickpeas.

Variation Tip: Use almond butter as a substitute of peanut butter.

Nutritional Information per Serving:
Calories: 354 | **Fat:** 20.5g | **Sodium:** 296mg | **Carbs:** 29.4g | **Fiber:** 5.6g | **Sugar:** 17.5g | **Protein:** 16.5g

Cauliflower Smoothie

Prep time: 10 minutes
Cook time: 00 minutes
Serves: 1

Ingredients:

- 1 cup soy milk
- 1 cup frozen cauliflower florets
- 1.5 tablespoons unsweetened cocoa powder
- 3 tablespoons flax seeds
- A pinch of sea salt

Preparation:

1. Put all ingredients into blender and blend until smooth.

Serving Suggestion: Serve the Cauliflower Smoothie with chips.

Variation Tip: You can use chia seeds as a substitute of flax seeds.

Nutritional Information per Serving:
Calories: 223 | **Fat:** 11.5g | **Sodium:** 510mg | **Carbs:** 20g | **Fiber:** 8.7g | **Sugar:** 9.1g | **Protein:** 13.5g

Pumpkin Spice Smoothie

Prep time: 10 minutes
Cook time: 00 minutes
Serves: 1

Ingredients:

- 1/2 cup unsweetened rice milk
- 1/2 cup pumpkin purée
- 2 tablespoon peanut butter
- ¼ teaspoon of pumpkin pie spice
- 1/2 cup ice
- A pinch of sea salt

Preparation:

1. Put all ingredients into blender and blend until smooth.

Serving Suggestion: Serve the Pumpkin Spice Smoothie with sandwich.

Variation Tip: Use almond butter as a substitute of peanut butter.

Nutritional Information per Serving:
Calories: 515 | **Fat:** 45g | **Sodium:** 264mg | **Carbs:** 22.9g | **Fiber:** 9.5g | **Sugar:** 9.5g | **Protein:** 10.9g

Lime Pie Smoothie

Prep time: 10 minutes
Cook time: 00 minutes
Serves: 1

Ingredients:

- 1 cup water
- ½ cup unsweetened coconut milk
- ¼ cup raw Peanuts
- 1 cup kale
- 2 tablespoon shredded coconut
- 2 tablespoon of lime juice

Preparation:

1. Put all ingredients into blender and blend until smooth.

Serving Suggestion: Serve the Lime Pie Smoothie with chips.

Variation Tip: Use cashew as a substitute of shredded coconut.

Nutritional Information per Serving:
Calories: 281 | **Fat:** 21.1g | **Sodium:** 130mg | **Carbs:** 22.2g | **Fiber:** 3.5g | **Sugar:** 4g | **Protein:** 7.3g

Coffee with Cream

Prep time: 10 minutes
Cook time: 00 minutes
Serves: 1

Ingredients:

- ¾ cup coffee, brewed the way you like it
- ¼ cup heavy whipping cream

Preparation:

1. Brew your coffee the way you like it best. Place the cream in a small saucepan and heat gently, stirring, until frothy.
2. Pour the lukewarm cream into a large mug, add the coffee and stir. Serve immediately or accompany with a handful of nuts or a piece of cheese.

Serving Suggestion: Serve the Coffee with Cream with any snacks.

Variation Tip: You can use coconut milk as a substitute of whipping cream.

Nutritional Information per Serving:
Calories: 105 | **Fat:** 11.1g | **Sodium:** 15mg | **Carbs:** 0.8g | **Fiber:** 0g | **Sugar:** 0g | **Protein:** 0.8g

Desserts Recipes

Chocolate Pudding Cake

Prep time: 10 minutes
Cook time: 35 minutes
Serves: 4

Ingredients:

- 6 tablespoons almond flour
- 6 tablespoons coconut sugar
- ¾ teaspoon baking powder
- ¼ teaspoon baking soda
- 1/8 teaspoon salt
- ½ cup unsweetened cocoa powder
- ¼ cup almond milk
- 1½ tablespoon unsalted butter melted
- ¾ teaspoon vanilla extract
- ¼ cup firmly packed brown sugar
- 1 cups boiling water
- Cooking spray
- Berries whipped cream and mint for garnish if desired.

Preparation:

1. Preheat the oven to 350° F. Butter a 9-inch square pan or round soufflé pan. Combine flour, coconut sugar, baking powder, baking soda, salt and 1/3 cup cocoa in a medium bowl. Add the milk, butter and vanilla and stir until combined. Pour the dough into the prepared shape.
2. Combine the brown sugar and remaining ¼ cup cocoa powder in a small bowl. Sprinkle evenly over the dough. Pour boiling water over all the mixture, do not stir.
3. Bake for 35 to 38 minutes until toothpick inserted in top layer comes out clean. Let it cool for at least ten minutes. Serve in bowls with garnishes if desired.

Serving Suggestion: Serve the Chocolate Pudding Cake with any chips.

Variation Tip: You can use coconut milk as a substitute of almond milk.

Nutritional Information per Serving:
Calories: 342 | **Fat:** 11.1g | **Sodium:** 257mg | **Carbs:** 46.8g | **Fiber:** 5.1g | **Sugar:** 10g | **Protein:** 6.3g

Almond Cookies

Prep time: 05 minutes
Cook time: 10 minutes
Serves: 4

Ingredients:

- ¼ cup almond flour
- ¼ cup coconut flour
- 2 scoops collagen peptides
- 1/8 cup honey
- 2 tablespoons melted coconut oil
- 1 teaspoon vanilla extract
- Pinch of sea salt

Preparation:

1. Preheat the oven to 350° F.
2. Combine the ingredients in a mixing bowl.
3. Divide the dough into eight balls and place them on a prepared baking sheet or silicone mat.
4. Bake for ten to 12 minutes, until the edges turn slightly brown.
5. Take the baking sheet out of the oven, then use the back of a fork to flatten the cookies into a cross shape.
6. Let the cookies cool a bit before serving.

Serving Suggestion: Serve the Almond Cookies with coffee.

Variation Tip: Use maple syrup as a substitute of honey.

Nutritional Information per Serving:
Calories: 138 | **Fat:** 6.9g | **Sodium:** 35mg | **Carbs:** 13.8g | **Fiber:** 1.5g | **Sugar:** 6g | **Protein:** 5.6g

Chocolate Raspberry Cheesecake

Prep time: 10 minutes
Cook time: 00 minutes
Serves: 12

Ingredients:

- 18 ounces reduced fat cream cheese, at room temperature
- 2/3 cup non-fat plain Greek yogurt
- 1/2 cup maple syrup
- ¼ cup unsweetened cocoa powder
- 2 large eggs
- 1 cup fresh raspberries divided
- 1/3 cup mini chocolate chips of choice

Preparation:

1. Preheat the oven to 280° F | 140° C. Pour boiling water halfway up a large deep casserole dish and place the pan on the lowest rack of the oven (this will keep the humidity in the oven and prevent the cheesecake from cracking deeply and does not dry out). Grease and line an 8-inch round removable cake pan. Put aside.
2. Combine cream cheese, yogurt and maple syrup in a bowl. Beat on low speed until smooth and combined. Stir in cocoa powder until incorporated into cream cheese mixture. Add eggs and beat again until smooth, about one minute.
3. Add 3/4 cup of the raspberries and 1/3 of the chocolate chips and gently fold in.
4. Pour into prepared cake pan. Cover with the remaining chocolate chips and bake for 40-50 minutes on the center bar of the oven until firm in the middle (there will still be a little sway in the middle). Turn off the oven and let the cheesecake cool slowly for about one hour with the oven door open.
5. After cooling, place on a wire rack to cool completely before covering and refrigerating for five to six hours or overnight.
6. To serve, garnish with remaining fresh raspberries and drizzle with melted chocolate.

Serving Suggestion: Serve the Chocolate Raspberry Cheesecake with any snacks.

Variation Tip: You can use any kind of sweetener.

Nutritional Information per Serving:

Calories: 89 | **Fat:** 5.8g | **Sodium:** 15mg | **Carbs:** 4g | **Fiber:** 1.3g | **Sugar:** 2g | **Protein:** 4.8g

Nut Fudge

Prep time: 10 minutes
Cook time: 00 minutes
Serves: 12

Ingredients:

- 1 ounce almond
- 1/8 cup coconut Milk
- 1 tablespoon cocoa powder (Unsweetened)
- 1/3 tablespoon maple syrup
- 1 scoop Chocolate Whey Protein
- 2 tablespoon almond butter

Preparation:

1. Mix all the ingredients with a hand blender/food processor, incorporate the nuts.
2. Cover the baking sheet with baking paper/cling film, fill the dough.
3. Freeze for an hour then chop into the desired shape! And it is ready to eat.

Serving Suggestion: Serve the Nut Fudge with any snacks.

Variation Tip: Use almond milk as a substitute of coconut milk.

Nutritional Information per Serving:
Calories: 54 | **Fat:** 2.8g | **Sodium:** 40mg | **Carbs:** 2.8g | **Fiber:** 0.7g | **Sugar:** 0.7g | **Protein:** 5.5g

Almond Graham Crackers

Prep time: 30 minutes
Cook time: 15 minutes
Serves: 11

Ingredients:

- 2¼ cups almond flour (divided)
- ¼ cup honey
- 1 teaspoon ground cinnamon
- ½ teaspoon baking soda
- ¼ teaspoon salt
- 2 tablespoons pure maple syrup
- 2 tablespoons Molasses
- 2 tablespoons Unsweetened Applesauce
- 2 tablespoons coconut oil
- 1 tablespoon unsweetened almond milk
- 1 teaspoon vanilla extract

Preparation:

1. Line two baking sheets with parchment paper and place a large silpat on your work surface.
2. Put a cup of almond flour in a small bowl.
3. In a medium bowl, combine the remaining 1½ cups almond flour, honey, cinnamon, baking soda and salt.
4. In a large bowl, combine the maple syrup, molasses, applesauce, oil, milk and vanilla extract. Pour the dry ingredients over the wet ingredients and stir in.
5. Sprinkle the remaining ¾ cup of reserved flour over the silpat and knead the dough. Once a ball forms, let the dough rest for ten minutes.
6. Preheat the oven to 350° Fahrenheit. Roll out the dough ~ ⅛ "thick. Cut the cookies with a pizza cutter and lift each square onto the prepared shape with a spatula. Flatten the dough with a fork, then bake for ~ 14-16 (time to baking depends on the biscuit from, just watch and remove the cookies when the edges are lightly browned). Slide baking paper onto the wire rack and let cool completely.

Serving Suggestion: Serve the Almond Graham Crackers with any coffee.

Variation Tip: Use coconut milk as a substitute of almond milk.

Nutritional Information per Serving:
Calories: 150 | **Fat:** 3g | **Sodium:** 85mg | **Carbs:** 28g | **Fiber:** 3g | **Sugar:** 10g | **Protein:** 3g

Lemon Coconut Protein Balls

Prep time: 05 minutes
Cook time: 35 minutes
Serves: 6

Ingredients:

- ¼ cup protein powder
- ¼ cup melted butter
- 6 tablespoon unsweetened shredded coconut
- 1 tablespoon maple syrup
- 1 tablespoon lemon juice + zest to taste
- 1 tablespoon almond flour

Preparation:

1. Combine the vanilla protein powder, melted butter, unsweetened coconut, maple syrup, lemon juice + lemon zest and flour, coconut in a mixing bowl.
2. Shape the dough into balls.
3. Place the balls in the refrigerator on a baking sheet lined with parchment paper for 30-45 minutes.
4. Serve immediately! Protein balls can be stored in an airtight container in the refrigerator for up to five days.

Serving Suggestion: Serve the Lemon Protein Balls with milk.

Variation Tip: Use honey as a substitute of maple syrup.

Nutritional Information per Serving:
Calories: 69 | **Fat:** 4.8g | **Sodium:** 19mg | **Carbs:** 5.8g | **Fiber:** 1.6g | **Sugar:** 3.4g | **Protein:** 1.1g

Berry Chocolate Mousses

Prep time: 10 minutes
Cook time: 00 minutes
Serves: 2

Ingredients:

- 1 large ripe avocado, frozen with the skin and stone removed
- 2 tablespoons cacao powder
- 3 tablespoons coconut cream
- ½ teaspoon vanilla extract
- ¼ teaspoon maple syrup
- ¼ raspberries
- 1 teaspoon shredded coconut

Preparation:

1. In a food processor, combine the frozen avocado, cocoa powder, coconut cream, vanilla extract and maple syrup until smooth.
2. Transfer to a bowl and gently add the raspberries.
3. Sprinkle grated coconut and serve.

Serving Suggestion: Serve the Berry Chocolate Mousses with any snacks

Variation Tip: Use stevia if you don't like maple syrup.

Nutritional Information per Serving:
Calories: 283 | **Fat:** 26.3g | **Sodium:** 10mg | **Carbs:** 14.5g | **Fiber:** 9.8g | **Sugar:** 2.1g | **Protein:** 3.6g

Almond Barley Pudding

Prep time: 20 minutes
Cook time: 40 minutes
Serves: 2

Ingredients:

- 1 teaspoon cinnamon
- 2 cardamom pods
- ½ tsp Allspice
- ½ cup barley
- ¾ cup soy milk
- ¾ tablespoon honey

Preparation:

1. Pour two cups of water, cinnamon, cardamom and Allspice into a medium saucepan.
2. Heat over medium heat and bring the liquid to a boil.
3. Add the barley after the liquid boils. Bring back to a boil and lower the heat, bring the mixture to a boil. Cook for 15 to 20 minutes or until the barley is tender.
4. Once the barley is cooked, turn off the heat and remove cardamom.
5. In another medium saucepan, heat the soy milk to a boil.
6. Add honey until combined. Then add the barley.
7. Simmer the mixture for seven to nine minutes. The mixture thickens as the liquid evaporates. Remove from the heat when the desired consistency of the pudding is reached.
8. Transfer to a bowl and garnish with toasted coconut.

Serving Suggestion: Serve the Almond Barley Pudding with any snacks.

Variation Tip: Use coconut milk as a substitute of soy milk.

Nutritional Information per Serving:
Calories: 695 | **Fat:** 48g | **Sodium:** 32mg | **Carbs:** 64.8g | **Fiber:** 12.3g | **Sugar:** 14.7g | **Protein:** 8g

Peanut Butter Protein Cookies

Prep time: 10 minutes
Cook time: 12 minutes
Serves: 12

Ingredients:

- 1 cup quick oats
- 2 scoops vanilla protein powder
- 1/2 cup peanut butter
- ¼ cup unsweetened mashed banana
- 2 tablespoons maple syrup

Preparation:

1. Preheat the oven to 350° F.
2. Place the oatmeal and protein powder in a small bowl and stir.
3. Combine peanut butter, mashed banana and maple syrup in a separate bowl. Pour the wet peanut butter mixture over the dry mixture and mix well. Combining this mixture requires some stirring strength and may seem a bit crumbly at first glance. I kneaded the dough with my hands towards the end and it seems to be helping. If it's too crumbly, you can add an additional one to two tablespoons of applesauce to moisten it.
4. After combining, begin shaping the dough into 1-inch balls.
5. Place the balls on a baking sheet lined with parchment paper, use a fork to press the balls into a cookie mold and bake for 12 minutes.
6. Take out of the oven, let cool and enjoy. Store leftovers in an airtight, covered container on the counter/fridge for immediate consumption or keep them in the freezer for later.

Serving Suggestion: Serve the Peanut Butter Protein Cookies with any coffee.

Variation Tip: Use honey as a substitute maple syrup.

Nutritional Information per Serving:
Calories: 107 | **Fat:** 6g | **Sodium:** 42mg | **Carbs:** 9g | **Fiber:** 2g | **Sugar:** 2g | **Protein:** 5g

Banana Protein Mug Cake

Prep time: 03 minutes
Cook time: 05 minutes
Serves: 1

Ingredients:

- ¼ cup chocolate protein powder
- 1 small extra ripe banana, mashed
- ¼ teaspoon baking powder
- 1 pinch sea salt
- 1 large egg

Preparation:

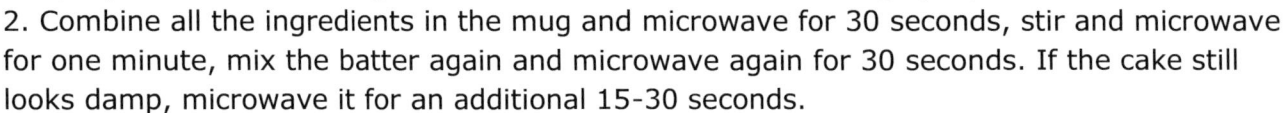

1. Spray a microwaved mug or small bowl with non-stick cooking spray.
2. Combine all the ingredients in the mug and microwave for 30 seconds, stir and microwave for one minute, mix the batter again and microwave again for 30 seconds. If the cake still looks damp, microwave it for an additional 15-30 seconds.
3. Enjoy directly from the cup or place on a small plate and garnish with fresh fruit, Greek yogurt, whipped cream and/or almond butter.

Serving Suggestion: Serve the Banana Protein Mug Cake with Greek yogurt.

Variation Tip: use applesauce if not using banana

Nutritional Information per Serving:
Calories: 210 | **Fat:** 0.5g | **Sodium:** 460mg | **Carbs:** 32.6g | **Fiber:** 4.2g | **Sugar:** 18.5g | **Protein:** 23g

Four Weeks Meal Plan

1st Week

Day	Breakfast	Lunch	Snacks	Dinner	Dessert
1	Overnight Oats	Lemon Basil Chicken	Lime Pie Smoothie	Ceviche	Almond Cookies
2	Frittata	Beef Cannelloni	Bacon Asparagus Bites	Cauliflower Fried Rice	Nut Fudge
3	Green Shakshuka	Roast Lamb	Jalapeño Popper Egg Cups	Moroccan Salmon	Banana Protein Mug Cake
4	Feta Egg Muffins	Chipotle Chicken Bowl	Coffee with Cream	Chickpeas Meatball	Chocolate Raspberry Cheesecake
5	Kale Mozzarella Wrap	Sweet Potato Chili	Cucumber Sushi	Korean Ground Beef	Chocolate Pudding Cake
6	Baked Eggs and Zoodles	Zucchini Noodles and Lemon Shrimp	Avocado Chips	Easy Turkey Salad	Berry Chocolate Mousses
7	Lime Poppy Seed Muffins	Sriracha BBQ Ground Beef and Green Beans	Cucumber Green Smoothie	Garlic Teriyaki Tempeh and Broccoli	Almond Barley Pudding

Second Week

Day	Breakfast	Lunch	Snacks	Dinner	Dessert
1	Frittata	Grilled Cauliflower Steak	Bacon Asparagus Bites	Simple Salmon chowder	Peanut Butter Protein Cookies
2	Green Shakshuka	Swiss chard & Artichoke Stuffed Pork Chops	Nutmeg Strawberries Smoothie	Lemon Basil Chicken	Banana Protein Mug Cake
3	Kale Mozzarella Wrap	Moroccan Salmon	Cucumber Sushi	Easy Turkey Salad	Lemon Coconut Protein Balls
4	Tempeh Scramble with Spinach and Carrots	Mushroom and Chicken	Burger Fat Bombs	Baked Cod with Tomatoes & Basil	Almond Graham Crackers
5	Feta Egg Muffins	Pork Chops with Warm Lemon Vinaigrette	Beet and Pumpkin Salad	Garlic Teriyaki Tempeh and Broccoli	Chocolate Raspberry Cheesecake
6	Egg and Veggie Breakfast Bowl	Roasted Mustard Seed White Fish	Pumpkin Spice Smoothie	Red Lentil Stew with Chickpeas	Almond Cookies
7	Tortilla with Zucchini	Sweet Ground Beef and Broccoli	Coconut blackberry Mint Smoothie	Tofu Stir-Fry	Nut Fudge

Third Week

Day	Breakfast	Lunch	Snacks	Dinner	Dessert
1	Baked Eggs and Zoodles	Pesto Chicken and Veggies	Avocado Chips	Baked Cod with Tomatoes & Basil	Nut Fudge
2	Lime Poppy Seed Muffins	Garlic Rosemary Pork Chops	Burger Fat Bombs	Tomato Quinoa Soup with Roasted Chickpeas	Almond Cookies
3	Tortilla with Zucchini	Lentil and Steak Salad	Bacon Asparagus Bites	Avocado Pesto Zucchini Noodles	Chocolate Pudding Cake
4	Egg and Veggie Breakfast Bowl	Swiss chard & Artichoke Stuffed Pork Chops	Cucumber Sushi	Spicy Shrimp and Sautéed Kale	Banana Protein Mug Cake
5	Kale Mozzarella Wrap	Turkey Burgers with Savory Warm Relish	Jalapeño Popper Egg Cups	Sweet Ground Beef and Broccoli	Berry Chocolate Mousses
6	Overnight Oats	Tofu Stir-Fry	Coffee with Cream	Beef Cannelloni	Almond Barley Pudding
7	Frittata	Turkey Parmesan Zucchini Boats	Cauliflower Smoothie	Grilled Cauliflower Steak	Lemon Coconut Protein Balls

Fourth Week

Day	Breakfast	Lunch	Snacks	Dinner	Dessert
1	Green Shakshuka	Sweet Potato Chili	Coffee with Cream	Roast Lamb	Berry Chocolate Mousses
2	Egg and Veggie Breakfast Bowl	Baked Salmon Recipe with Asparagus & Yogurt Dill Sauce	Lime Pie Smoothie	Lemon Basil Chicken	Lemon Coconut Protein Balls
3	Lime Poppy Seed Muffins	Easy Turkey Salad	Nutmeg Strawberries Smoothie	Sweet and Sour Tuna	Almond Graham Crackers
4	Frittata	Garlic Rosemary Pork Chops	Chocolate Peanut Butter Smoothie	Tomato Quinoa Soup with Roasted Chickpeas	Nut Fudge
5	Tortilla with Zucchini	Swiss chard & Artichoke Stuffed Pork Chops	Strawberry Zucchini Hemp Smoothie	Quick and Easy Salmon Cakes	Chocolate Raspberry Cheesecake
6	Baked Eggs and Zoodles	Mushroom and Chicken	Coconut Blackberry Mint Smoothie	Ceviche	Almond Cookies
7	Overnight Oats	Chipotle Chicken Bowl	Pumpkin spice Smoothie	Beans and Chicken Stir-Fry	Chocolate Pudding Cake

Conclusion

Before we dive into planning a Macro Diet program, we must first understand what macros are and how they affect our bodies. Macros, also called macronutrients (not to be confused with micronutrients), are molecules that we all need in large quantities to survive. The top three macronutrients we all focus on and rely on are carbohydrates, protein, and fat.

They work as follows:

Carbohydrates are the main source of energy for the body. Once consumed, they are broken down and turned into glucose, which the body and organs use to perform their daily functions.

Protein is known as the building blocks of bodybuilding, but it can do more. This macronutrient is responsible for building organs and bones, regulating metabolism, and maintaining a neutral environment by preventing inflammation that often leads to disease.

Fats – Contrary to popular belief, not all fats are bad for you. Good fats energize your body, promote cell growth, act as a protective layer around your organs, keep you warm, and help your body absorb certain nutrients and produce vital hormones among many other functions.

An important fact to keep in mind is that while the Macro Diet Plan monitors your macronutrient intake, that does not mean that micronutrients should be fuzzy and should not be consumed. Remember that micronutrient deficiencies often lead to impaired immune and visual function, poor physical and cognitive development, and increased risk of anemia and death.

Micronutrients, also called vitamins and minerals, are easily found in food sources like fruits, vegetables, legumes, whole grains and lean protein sources, as well as vitamin D and healthy fats like vegetables, nuts and olive oil.

Understand how many macros you need and in what proportion.

National dietary guidelines suggest that you should consume your macronutrient in the following proportions:

45 to 60% carbohydrates

20 to 35% fat

10 to 35% protein

Please note that these are recommendations intended for the general population. You can change the percentage depending on the diet you want. For example, a person on a high protein diet might eat the following servings: 25% carbohydrate, 35% fat, and 40% protein. It all depends on your individual preferences.

Printed in Great Britain
by Amazon